The Impact of
Microprocessors
on the
Small Accounting Practice

RESEARCH STUDIES IN ACCOUNTING
B.V. CARSBERG, SERIES EDITOR

Bhaskar, K.N., Williams, B.C.
**THE IMPACT OF MICROPROCESSORS
ON THE SMALL ACCOUNTING PRACTICE**

Bromwich, M.
**THE ECONOMICS OF ACCOUNTING
STANDARD SETTING**

Carsberg, B.V., Page, M.J. (Joint Editors)
CURRENT COST ACCOUNTING

Carsberg, B.V., Page, M.J., Sindall, A.J., Waring, I.D.
SMALL COMPANY FINANCIAL REPORTING

Glynn, J.J.
**VALUE FOR MONEY AUDITING
IN THE PUBLIC SECTOR**

Kirkman, P.R.A.
**INFLATION ACCOUNTING IN
MAJOR ENGLISH-SPEAKING COUNTRIES**

Macve, R.
SURVEY OF LLOYDS SYNDICATE ACCOUNTS

The Impact of Microprocessors on the Small Accounting Practice

K.N. BHASKAR
and
B.C. WILLIAMS
University of East Anglia

RESEARCH STUDIES IN ACCOUNTING
SERIES EDITOR: B.V. CARSBERG

Prentice-Hall International

Englewood Cliffs, N.J.   London   Mexico   New Delhi
Rio de Janeiro   Singapore   Sydney   Toronto   Wellington

in association with

THE INSTITUTE OF
CHARTERED
ACCOUNTANTS

IN ENGLAND & WALES

Library of Congress Cataloging in Publication Data

Bhaskar, Krish N.
  The impact of microprocessors on the small accounting
practice.

  (Research studies in accounting)
  Bibliography: p.
  1. Accounting——Data processing   2. Microcomputers
——Programming   3. Minicomputers——Programming
I. Williams, Bernard C.   II. Title.   III. Series.
  HF5679.B45 1986   657'.028'5416   85-25764
  ISBN 0-13-453291-0

British Library Cataloguing in Publication Data

Bhaskar, Krish
  The impact of microprocessors on the small accounting
practice.——(Research studies in accounting)
  1. Accounting——Data processing
  2. Microcomputers
  I. Title   II. Williams, B.C.   III. Institute of Chartered
Accountants in England and Wales
  IV. Series
  657'.028'5404   HF 5679

  ISBN 0-13-453291-0

*This book consists of a research study undertaken on behalf of
The Institute of Chartered Accountants in England and Wales.
In publishing this book the Institute considers that it is a
worthwhile contribution to discussion but neither the Institute
nor the Research Board necessarily shares the views expressed,
which are those of the authors alone.*

*No responsibility for loss occasioned to any person acting or
refraining from action as a result of any material in this publication
can be accepted by the authors or publisher.*

Prentice-Hall, Inc., *Englewood Cliffs, New Jersey*
Prentice-Hall International, (UK), Ltd, *London*
Prentice-Hall of Australia Pty Ltd, *Sydney*
Prentice-Hall Canada, Inc., *Toronto*
Prentice-Hall Hispanoamericana, S.A., *Mexico*
Prentice-Hall of India Private Ltd, *New Delhi*
Prentice-Hall of Japan, Inc., *Tokyo*
Prentice-Hall of Southeast Asia Pte Ltd, *Singapore*
Editora Prentice-Hall do Brasil Ltda, *Rio de Janeiro*
Whitehall Books Ltd, *Wellington, New Zealand*

*Printed and bound in Great Britain for
Prentice-Hall International (UK) Ltd.,
68 Wood Lane End, Hemel Hempstead HP2 4RG,
by A. Wheaton & Co. Ltd, Exeter*

1 2 3 4 5   90 89 88 87 86

ISBN 0-13-453291-0

This book
is dedicated to
Fenella and May

Contents

Foreword

Undoubtedly one of the most important forces for change in the business environment in recent years has been the revolution which has taken place in information technology and information processing. Computerised accounting systems have become more common, more complex and more powerful, and the implications for accounting have been widespread. Computer technology has been made available to even the smallest business, through the development of inexpensive microcomputers with processing power equivalent to their much larger and more costly predecessors. Accountants have sometimes been unsure whether to regard these developments as an opportunity or a threat. The accounting profession has had to respond to constant changes in technology, but the pace and nature of these changes have often made an adequate response difficult.

In this study, Krish Bhaskar and Bernard Williams are clear that information technology provides a great opportunity to accountants. The development of microprocessors, in particular, has opened up that opportunity to small accounting practices. The resources that such firms have available to make the preparations needed to take advantage of the rapid changes in technology are normally scarce and the help provided by the Bhaskar and Williams report will therefore be a considerable asset to practitioners. The study is of value both because it makes the small practice its main subject and also because it covers the dual aspects of the practitioner's response to the use of microprocessors in clients' businesses and the practitioner's use of microprocessors in his own work. Bhaskar and Williams try to provide practical help with respect to both hardware and software.

In the rapidly changing environment of information technology, this report provides encouragement to accountants to see the potential of computers as a means of enhancing the service provided to their clients and thus of ensuring the development of their own accounting practices.

Professor Bryan Carsberg
Director of Research
ICAEW

Preface

At the University of East Anglia, we are in the fortunate position of having sufficient resources to specialise in the study of computer applications in accountancy. In the context of the Information Technology revolution, the University has pioneered the use of new technology in the field of accounting, using a wide range of computer facilities and the specialised expertise of staff and research workers. These resources have been fully utilised in the production of this report.

The business community and the accounting profession are awakening to the rapidly accelerating pace of new developments in the IT revolution. They are becoming aware that the rapid changes now occurring require a vigorous response.

Small practices, the central objects of our study, are already gaining experience in the use of microcomputers and we will attempt to determine whether the computer can be a means of enhancing the degree of control exercised over the accounts of small businessses. We believe that greater control *can* be achieved, using the hardware and software solutions described in the report.

Computers can introduce greater discipline into the recording of economic transactions and, in association with software which enforces procedures such as the use of passwords and security copying, can greatly improve internal control. Hardware and software can thus provide the best compromise between allowing small businesses to remain flexible and innovative in their use of computers and retaining a degree of control which is acceptable to the accountant.

The second major theme of this report is the potential use of computers by small practices themselves, as aids to administration and as a means of generating new fee income. A positive response to the new technology is, we believe, vital – if small accountancy practices are to take advantage of this growth area and to prosper in the future.

It is evident that the profession has been deficient in its response to technological developments. An analogy with the medical profession might be appropriate; when faced with the problem of defining the point of death of a potential donor for a transplant operation, the medical profession responded quickly with suitable guidelines. By contrast, the accounting profession has been slow to face the problems raised by the use of information technology (first introduced some 30 years ago). Moreover, information technology is continually affecting the commercial community at an ever-accelerating rate. The Institute has, however, become more aware of the challenge to be faced and is taking an increasingly active role.

Nevertheless, action is urgently needed to develop the skills of professional accountants over a range of new activities. For the profession to remain passive would be tantamount to the surrender of accountancy's traditional areas of operation to others (e.g. the government, the data processing profession and the British Computer Society). The survival of the large international accounting firms is not in question, but what we believe is at risk is the survival of the smaller practice and, perhaps, the reputation and credibility of the profession as a whole.

If insufficient action is taken, either by the profession or by small practices, it is our belief that there is a strong likelihood of the disappearance of the one-man practitioner and the smaller practice. If this happens, a possible scenario is that the resulting oligarchy led by the larger accounting firms may be perceived as detrimental to business in the UK and its continued existence may be threatened.

The reasons for the vulnerability of the smaller practice are threefold:

1. Lack of expertise will lead to a service which is more costly than necessary (we have argued that computers can lower practice administration and increase productivity).
2. The smaller practice will be unable to offer a wider range of services and thus be unable to attract a higher fee income to offset its fixed overheads.
3. The profession may find itself in a position in which the small practice may lose its standing with its clients and with the general public.

We fear that the smaller practice might thus lose its competitive edge on cost grounds or revenue-generating grounds and lose credibility. Whilst the medium sized firm can, and has, recovered some of the lost ground, the small practice may lack the necessary resources.

Acknowledgements

The authors gratefully acknowledge the help of Paul Gardner, Mark Barry, Martyn Farnworth, Helen Clark, Martin Rix, Maureen Edmonds, Elaine Standen, Pam Sinclair and Gill Atkinson in the preparation of this report, but accept final responsibility for any errors or omissions.

K.N. Bhaskar
B.C. Williams
University of
East Anglia

Executive summary

INTRODUCTION

This executive summary has been compiled to enable the reader to scan the report quickly. The structure of the summary mirrors the main report, being a distillation of each of the main points. The reader is requested to refer to the main report for clarification, explanation or expansion of any points.

COMPUTER AUDITING IN THE SMALL BUSINESS ENVIRONMENT: CONCEPTS AND ISSUES

Essentially there are two types of auditing undertaken by the profession. These are as follows:

1. Auditing for true and fair purposes.
2. Value for money and other auditing.

This section is concerned primarily with the impact of the computer on true and fair audits of small companies with small business systems, on the assumption that the smaller practices do not audit a significant number of large clients.

There are a number of alternative approaches to the audit of a small business system. They include:

1. A practice approaches the audit of a small business system by 'auditing around the computer'.
2. A practice may qualify the audit of a small business system, rather than becoming involved in the small business machine.
3. A practice may carry out a systems-based audit. In this case adequate controls of the computer based system must be present.
4. A more radical approach of changing the auditing requirement of a

small business, for example, instead of an 'audit' a lower level of certification may be given such as a 'review'.

5.   A novel approach is for the practice to offer what is essentially an electronic data processing bureau service and undertake the processing of the firm's clients' accounts.

6.   Reprocessing the complete transaction files generated by the client's system.

Approaches 1 to 6 are discussed in Chapter 2. The theme of controls is further discussed in Chapters 3 and 4. Chapter 4 also deals with approach 6 and event accounting systems.

COMPUTER AUDIT APPROACHES AND TECHNIQUES

As will be noted in Chapter 2, the general approach to auditing through a computer is to carry out a systems-based audit. It is interesting to speculate whether a small to medium sized practice should carry out such an audit, which would involve an examination of the internal controls (including computer controls) operating in a company. One school of thought believes that systems based auditing is irrelevant for a small client; internal controls outside the computer system would be impracticable and costly to implement and systems controls inside the computer may be circumvented by someone with sufficient knowledge. This viewpoint is critically examined together with a set of conditions, including new technological solutions which may make this type of auditing relevant for small clients.

Approach found within the profession

The APC draft Auditing Guideline 'Auditing in a computer environment' made no general comment in relation to internal controls. The auditing guideline on computer assisted audit techniques distinguished small computers by remarking 'Where the enterprise uses a small computer the general principles in this guideline are still appropriate'.

Various approaches found within the profession are outlined in this chapter, including:

1.   Reliance on internal controls generally.

2.   Reliance on specific aspects of internal controls.

3.   Reliance on the integrity of the computer programs themselves.

INTERNAL CONTROL IN THE SMALL COMPUTERISED BUSINESS

Relevance of internal controls

Given that the practitioner has the necessary expertise and ability to follow through a computer audit, the next question to be raised is the relevance and usefulness of computer controls in a small business.

It is our opinion that new hardware and software solutions, described in Chapter 4, offer the best way forward. They offer the most secure internal controls within a small business environment and although there is a small 'imposition' on the actions of the personnel running the system (i.e. the owner), this infringement of individual liberty is minimised (the machine does most of the control) and the advantages of the micro – approachability, flexibility and freedom – are retained. Yet the accountant receives a higher standard of control than ever before in a small business context.

One of the objectives of this report has been to pose the question: can the Profession, by means of the introduction of the microprocessor, be offered a degree of control where none was possible? The answer is: yes, it can. The hardware and software solutions in Chapter 4 do just that. This may create, however, the need for the Profession to make a major step forward in the auditing of small businesses.

SMALL COMPUTER APPLICATIONS IN THE OFFICE OF THE SMALL BUSINESS AND THE SMALL PRACTICE

Formerly, most small organisations relied on manual accounting methods; some were making use of computer bureaus, others visible record computers and some were using mechanical accounting machines. Now that the cost of small computers has fallen so dramatically, more and more small organisations are installing their own 'in house' computers and fewer are relying on the other methods.

The installation of small computers within the smaller organisations will undoubtedly have an impact, which is likely to differ from that made by the installation of large computers in larger organisations. The reasons for this are the different characteristics of both small organisations and small computers, as considered in Chapter 1.

CASE STUDIES

During the course of the project, a number of small firms of practising accountants were visited. The case studies reported in Chapter 6 are representative of a wider cross-section of those firms.

The experiences of six different practices are documented in this section and it is hoped that this will prove useful to firms considering computerisation and provide comfort to those that have already embarked on that course.

The practices vary from the medium size practice down to the sole practitioner, three are based in London and three are provincial firms.

OPPORTUNITIES TO ASSIST CLIENTS AND IMPROVE PRODUCTIVITY

A major way in which clients may be helped is through the pegging or lowering of fees for the provision of standard services. The features described below are aimed at reducing costs and/or increasing productivity with this aim in mind. The level and quality of service may also improve. The accounting firm which, through the use of technology, can offer a better service at a lower cost will have a distinct advantage over its less innovative competitor.

Cost reduction and productivity
In trying to provide a framework for the practitioner, the following list of areas open to increased efficiency may be useful:

1. General electronic communication facilities for offices.
2. Word processing of letters. Individual letters which can be sent to all clients or categories of clients.
3. A second type of word processing (plus memory capabilities) involving such items as accounts preparation, tax return schedules and possibly the tax return itself.
4. Other potential long run cost-saving devices in connection with tax returns are:
    (a) Building society and bank interest received could be accessed direct from the building society or bank computer via data communications through the telephone network – though this poses problems of confidentiality.
    (b) A similar operation could be performed for dividends using a hypothetical central dividend record scheme – this also poses problems of confidentiality.
    (c) Calculations for tax and other decisions (e.g. the splitting of a husband's and wife's tax assessment) could be performed.
    (d) A data bank and information retrieval function on tax law (including cases) and recently accepted practice by various tax offices could also be recorded, either via a Prestel-type service or

some other central databank. The information could be down-loaded to a floppy disc which would be regularly updated.

5. The recording of the accounting firm's own records.
6. The use of a microprocessor in a decision support role to help the accounting firm.
7. Manpower planning systems and work scheduling.
8. However (7) above is not sufficient. A firm needs to know the profitability of individual staff (and categories of staff) as well as the profitability of individual types of work.
   (*Note:* the potential for (7) and (8) in the very small practice is slight.)
9. Some of the items developed previously could be extended: for example, the creation of databanks on client's tax and financial information.

New fee income opportunities

Some examples of these new services and functions are considered, including:

* Assistance in the purchase and installation of small business systems.
* Data processing bureau work.
* Financial director or consultant role.
* Decision support systems.
* Referral and sub-contract work.
* Communication and office facilities.

To put the sources of fee income in context, it is quite conceivable that within ten years, the bulk of the fee income from a practice could be derived from these new sources.

CONCLUSIONS

Areas of interest for the profession

There are four central issues for the Profession:

1. The audit of small businesses and the meaning, level and standard of that audit (see Chapters 2 and 3).
2. The level of expertise with respect to computer knowledge of the Institute of Chartered Accountants in England and Wales (ICAEW) member (see Chapters 2 to 8).
3. The way in which practices operate their internal administration (see Chapters 5 and 6).
4. The range of services offered by a professional practice to its clients (see Chapters 5 to 7).

What we have done
In the course of this investigation we have identified the major problems
and research areas and become familiar with similar research activity
worldwide. We have undertaken a number of case studies of small
practices and performed a limited amount of experimental research.

RECOMMENDATIONS

Having outlined the very real dangers, which we do not believe have
been overstated, our recommendations to the Profession are given in
Appendix 1. Other recommendations and policy issues are discussed in
later chapters.

1

Introduction

INTRODUCTION

This project, sponsored by the Institute of Chartered Accountants in England and Wales, has four main aims. These are:

1. To identify major problems involved in using microprocessors and to review related research both in the UK and worldwide.
2. To carry out a limited number of case studies of smaller practices which have installed small computers.
3. To carry out a limited amount of experimental research.
4. To provide:
   - (a) A summary of the latest developments in the impact of the micro-processor on the small business system.
   - (b) An analysis of future research needs in the area.
   - (c) Suggestions for conferences, seminars and the content of a general educational programme to make the small practice more aware of the opportunities created and the problems associated with the new microprocessor-based technology.

The impact of the microprocessor has been examined from the viewpoints of the practice and the client. The work undertaken by the typical small practice is broad and varied. To keep the scope of the project within reasonable bounds, it has been restricted primarily to questions of accounting and auditing. Other areas of work, such as taxation, are mentioned briefly but are not considered in detail. However, it has been difficult to avoid wider areas since a practice is a business and it can therefore utilise the computer revolution both to increase efficiency across the range of its existing activities and to generate new sources of revenue.

An immediate and obvious problem that faces the profession is computer literacy and the education gap. At present school children are becoming computer-literate, accepting and handling computers as a matter of course. At universities, computers are often used in science and social science subjects and even in some humanities subjects. Up to 25 years will elapse before some of these children and students occupy positions of influence in the profession and are capable of directing developments. Meanwhile, if new opportunities are to be realised, those currently in such positions should be prepared to encourage and accept computerisation and its consequences wholeheartedly.

In the past the profession has been slow to encourage the study of basic accounting theory, preferring to concentrate on more pragmatic issues. The profession must not content itself with pragmatic solutions to problems posed by computers but must adopt the positive, constructive, and enquiring approach which alone can reap dividends in the future (see for example Chapter 6, Practice 2, p.79, – savings on future labour costs).

The arrival of plentiful, cheap and accessible computing power, as provided by the microprocessor, should be the answer to every accountant's dream, because it enables all the processing of transactions to be performed at the touch of a button. Although many practitioners are aware of the potential, the education gap is still very great. Admittedly, on the negative side, computerisation may produce additional control problems (as do all powerful objects); but on the positive side, the computer has the power to reduce the emphasis on detail and leave the accountant free to concentrate on more important issues, decisions and enquiries.

This line of thought prompts a number of key questions that are related to the impact of small computers on the small practice. These can be summarised as follows:

1. How can the advent of computer power under the direct control of a small practice be harnessed to serve its clients more efficiently? (See Chapters 5-7.)
2. How can small practices ensure that they maintain the technical competence and qualifications required to meet their professional and legal responsibilities whilst recognising and accepting the challenge of the small computer? (See Chapters 2-7.)
3. Will the use of small computers significantly affect client internal control given that the sheer variety of hardware, software, environment and relative cost has militated against the development of computer-assisted audit techniques (CAAT) for the small computer? (See Chapters 2, 3, and Appendix 3.)
4. What effect is the introduction of small computers having on standards and practices? (Chapter 3.)

5. What efforts are being made by the profession to close the wide gap that exists between the development and the use of information technology? (Chapter 7.)

Report outline
Chapter 2 examines the concepts and issues involved in computer auditing in the small business environment. The possible approaches are classified under six headings.

General computer audit approaches and techniques are then introduced in Chapter 3, leading to a discussion of the implications of the gap between large company audit techniques and the requirements of the small company.

Chapter 4 deals with the question of internal control in the small computerised business. As well as providing a brief introduction to internal controls in computer based accounting systems, this Chapter questions the relevance and usefulness of currently accepted controls and gives some suggestions for newer and less restrictive ones.

An examination of the uses of computers in the office of the small organisation follows in Chapter 5, including some speculation about likely future developments. This section concludes by examining the impact of the small computer on the activities of the smaller accounting practice.

Chapter 6 contains details of the specific impact that computerisation has had on a limited sample of varying types of small practice.

Chapter 7 considers positive ways in which the small computer can assist the small practice both in terms of increasing its own productivity and assisting its clients. General conclusions are contained in Chapter 8 with policy recommendations in Appendix 1.

Microprocessors
The terms microprocessor, microcomputer and microcomputer systems are often used incorrectly. At this stage in the report it is worth defining these terms to prevent future misunderstandings. The term microprocessor can be understood by looking at its ever-increasing rate of development on a decade-by-decade basis.

1950   Arrival of transistor – first use of semi conductor chips as opposed to valves.

1960   Arrival of integrated circuit – more than one transistor per chip.

1970   Large scale integration chips arrive – possible to place 100 transistors on one chip and thus to maintain certain computer circuits capable of performing simple operations on one chip.

1980 Advanced microprocessor chips available – 10000 transistors possible on one chip. A single chip capable of running a computer.

Without the development of semi-conductor transistor technology, the construction and operation of present day computers would have been impossible.

All present day computers make use of microprocessors but it is only the smaller computers that tend to rely on a single chip as the central processing unit. The central processing unit of larger computers will comprise several chips or microprocessors in order to obtain faster operating speeds.

Microcomputers therefore generally rely on one microprocessor chip which is responsible for the computer's operating capabilities. Surprisingly, it is not the traditional computing giants who produce these chips but a handful of independent companies.

Generally, users are not concerned with the type of microprocessor incorporated in any particular microcomputer. They simply need to know how to give instructions to the computer, using procedures incorporated in what is known as software. However, just as some rudimentary knowledge about the mechanics of a motor car is useful for assessment of its likely performance, so some knowledge of microprocessors will help users to assess the characteristics of a microcomputer.

One important difference among microprocessors is in the distinction between 8-bit and 16-bit chips (some early microprocessor chips were 4-bit and 32-bit chips are currently under development). This distinction determines how information is carried and processed within the chip.

With an 8-bit chip, information is carried in packages of 8 binary digits at a time, similarly a 16-bit chip allows information to be carried in packages of 16 binary digits. This means that 16-bit microprocessors can process a given amount of data faster and allow greater security by reducing the probability of data corruption. In addition, a 16-bit microprocessor is able to access a larger internal memory, allowing larger programs to be run.

As mentioned earlier, the user operates a microprocessor with the help of software. Software falls broadly into two categories: operating systems and applications software. The operating system performs administrative and caretaking functions (e.g. loading programs from disks), whereas applications software is used for performing specific tasks (e.g. sales ledger programs and nominal ledger programs). The choice of microprocessor will affect the choice of operating system which in turn dictates which application software packages can be run on a particular microcomputer system. (Some examples of microcomputer systems, operating systems and applications software are given in Appendix 2.)

Small business systems

Small computers, in common with larger computers, are all based on the same logical design. This is illustrated in Figure 1.1 and comprises input; output, processing and storage devices. Also given below are the choices that are normally available for each of the constituent parts of a typical small business system. (Note that K usually denotes thousands: 500K bytes means approximately 500,000 characters of storage, whilst 5 megabytes is approximately 5 million characters of storage. Main memory can be accessed quickly whilst files of information requiring slower access are held on disc. VDU stands for visual display unit.)

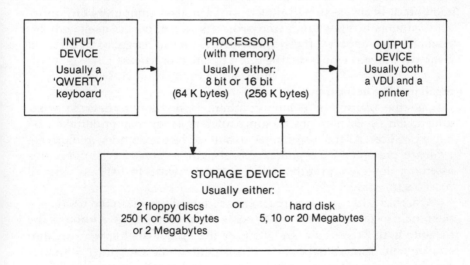

Figure 1.1 Possible microcomputer systems.

Much has been written about the distinctions among the definitions of mainframe, mini and microcomputer systems. Initially, much of the discussion focussed on cost; a typical example notes that: Mainframes cost over £20,000, minis from £7,500 to £100,000, and microcomputers £40 to £10,000. More recently, Bodnar (1980) advanced an alternative means of distinction. He suggested that minicomputers were descendants of mainframe machines and were supplied by the computing giants largely on a system-oriented basis. By contrast, microcomputers evolved from calculators, were made by small and hitherto unknown companies and were sold on a machine-oriented basis. However, this definition has become less apt with the passage of time. Today, the computer giants are making and selling microcomputers (such as the IBM Personal Computer and DEC Rainbow) and many of the original microcomputer manufacturers have become large mature companies (for example Apple and Commodore). Perhaps a more meaningful definition is the one given at a recent British Computer Society meeting, 'If it is airconditioned, it is a mainframe; if it stands on the floor, it is a mini, and if it sits on a desk, it is a microcomputer'!

Indeed distinctions among the three categories of computers change with the passage of time and boundaries become blurred. To avoid such difficulties, this project avoids the selection of a narrowly defined category of computers as its focus and considers instead those systems which are likely to be used by either small practices or their clients. In addition, it is also assumed that only 'in house' computers are under consideration. In other words, the project does not concern itself with, for example, the impact of the microprocessor on large computers in computer bureaus which may be used by small practices.

Small practice definition

Despite the paucity of evidence, there is no doubt that the work undertaken by smaller practices is different from that undertaken by larger practices. All the case studies examined by the authors, and private evidence presented by a good cross-section of practices, support this assertion. However, no authoritative definition exists to distinguish small practices from large.

Apart from the very large practices, accounting firms in the UK do not publish financial statements or statistics about themselves. Although the Institute in its literature acknowledges the existence of small, medium and large practices it makes no attempt to define these categories other than by the number of partners. Some researchers (Briston and Williams (1981)) have examined this problem of definition but have made little headway. Many institute members would consider a small practice to be one that had up to 1,000 clients, about £500,000 gross fees and about 5 partners, with a medium practice being up to about 10,000 clients and gross fees between £500,000-£3m. However, no firm quantitative or qualitative definitions have arisen so far.

Thus for the purposes of the report, it is necessary to look for a soft system of classification in the manner of the Bolton Report on Small Firms (1971) (see below). The Bolton report makes use of organisational and operating characteristics rather than pure physical characteristics like gross fees per annum, number of partners and so on.

For the purposes of this report, a small practice is regarded as one with the following characteristics:

1. No specialist service functions are available: for example no tax department (though the work of a practice may be heavily tax orientated), no research and technical department, no trust department, and no computing department.
2. All partners and any qualified staff are expected to have a working knowledge of all aspects of a chartered accountant's job, although some specialisation is usual.
3. The majority of work comprises the provision of accounting services and/or tax services to small businesses or individuals.
4. Few, if any, clients listed on the Stock Exchange.

Appendix 6 contains descriptions of six practices that were visited during the course of the project and which are featured as case studies in Chapter 6. Some of the practices could be considered as medium sized on the grounds of gross fees and other similar criteria, but broadly speaking, their characteristics conform to the above definitions.

Small business definition

The final definition needed for the project is of small businesses. There is no single definition which adequately identifies a small business. A variety of physical characteristics may be used. For example, the Companies Act 1981 (heavily influenced by the EEC Fourth Directive on Company Law Harmonisation) defines three categories of company as follows:

	Small	*Medium*	*Large*
Turnover	Does not exceed £1.4m	Does not exceed £5.75m	Any two
Balance sheet totals	Does not exceed £0.7m	Does not exceed £2.8m	items above
Average no. of employees	Does not exceed 50	Does not exceed 250	these limits

The basic rule is that no two conditions should be exceeded in either the current year or the preceding year.

In its interim report, the Wilson Committee (1979) gave a range of definitions of small businesses in different industries, but it recognised the limitations of such definitions. The committee argued that it did not want its recommendations based solely on its definition of a small business, and accepted that no precise definitions were entirely satisfactory.

Concrete definitions are obligatory in legal documents in order that the law may be objective; however, their inherent rigidity does not make them a particularly useful way of describing a firm with a view to understanding the way it operates, its problems and its attributes. The Bolton Report on Small Firms (1971) produces a more useful definition and describes the small firm as follows:

(a) It has a relatively small share of its market.
(b) It is managed by its owners or part-owners in a personalised way (i.e. the owners actively participate in all aspects of management to a great degree).
(c) It is independent of outside control in principal decision-taking.

More recently, Mackness (1975) has suggested that a small firm is characterised by the following:

(a) Lack of specialist services to advise management.
(b) The necessity for senior people to get involved in all aspects of running the business.
(c) The involvement of only one or two people in significant decision-taking.
(d) Lack of time for senior people to think about development of the firm.

These ideas have since gained wider acceptance with the definition which appears in para 2.2 of UEC draft auditing statement No. 13 (1982). It regards a small firm as one in which:

(a) Management is in the hands of one or a few people who combine all or most of the essential functions of marketing, manufacturing, personnel, finance and accounting.
(b) Management and their families own all or a large part of the enterprise.
(c) Because of its talents and ownership, management dominates the enterprise in all essential aspects.
(d) The owner/manager is generally involved in many of the day-to-day operations.
(e) The small number of employees limits the possibility of an adequate segregation of functions.

(f) From an accounting point of view, the systems tend to be relatively uncomplicated.

Although these definitions are less objective than the legal versions, they do describe more accurately the nature of small businesses. They are also much more useful when trying to assess management information requirements which will be based on organisational structure and relationships with the outside world. In other words; the impact, choice and use of computer systems and hence equipment will depend on a behavioural classification rather than a legal classification.

Implications

The characteristics of both small practices and small businesses are important because they show that both the accountant in practice and his clients' personnel have no experts to turn to for advice when considering computerisation. Whereas the client may quite rightly consider turning to his professional accountant as a source of information and advice, the practising accountant will not be in a position to provide guidance. The latter has a professional duty to be technically competent in the area of computerised accountancy just as he is expected to be competent and fully conversant with subjects like accounting standards and double-entry book-keeping.

The majority of small practices fail to satisfy the requirement for competence in computerised accounting. Typically in small practices it is a young partner who will provide the impetus and enthusiasm for the installation of in-house computing facilities and generally the majority of the partners will not be computer-literate or indeed capable of providing advice to clients on computerisation. We feel that professional firms should take the lead in computerised accountancy rather than wait for external pressures to force them into this area.

Interestingly, the Wilson Committee (1979), in its Interim Report, (Recommendation 12, Appendix 2) recommended that the accountancy bodies should take steps to ensure that their members are both equipped and encouraged to take a more active role in providing adequate advice to their smaller business clients.)

Small business systems – the state of the art

Currently there is a dramatic increase in the use of small computers and in particular, in their use as small business systems. Within the market place there are many different manufacturers and distributors active in this area. Unfortunately, potential customers not only face the bewildering array of systems subject to various claims, counter-claims and uncertain continuity, but in addition are unsure of what can be achieved by this new technology. This uncertainty arises through a lack of general awareness of information technology and an inability (caused by a lack of independent or non-commercial literature) to find out precisely what can and cannot be achieved by its use.

Manufacturers of large machines are trying to break into markets formerly held by manufacturers of small machines whilst the latter are trying desperately to reverse this process. The battle is chiefly being fought, at the meeting point of these two forces, around 16-bit machines (i.e. machines with 16-bit central processing unit chips).

Future plans currently being implemented by computer manufacturers envisage the development and use of 32-bit chips and hence 32-bit microcomputers. However, technological developments are far in advance of applications. There is a wealth of software available in the 8-bit microcomputer field and it is apparent that there is still much more potential development in this area. Commercial pressures portray 16-bit machines as being the next generation of microcomputers; however the step up from 8-bit machines is small compared with that which is required to move from a manual system to a computerised system.

The popularisation of small computers and desk-top computers in particular was predicted to have a dramatic effect on the organisation and structure of many enterprises. This has been found to be true in many of the firms studied in this project. It has given rise to what may be called 'Personal Computer Power' which in turn has led to a degree of 'EDP anarchy'. It is possible today, in large firms, to buy quite powerful computers, well below observable and controllable capital expenditure limits. Whilst this has had the undeniable advantage of placing the decision-maker and user of information in close contact with a computer it has also encouraged the user to disregard EDP guidelines when acquiring his or her own computer. If a business has various different kinds of computers, organisational consequences such as lack of portability of software and an inability to form networks may arise.

In the small practice or among its clients, such problems are rarely faced since these types of organisation usually have decision-making concentrated in the hands of one or two people and in addition it is unlikely that they would have a specialist department such as an EDP department.

Small practitioners or their clients (usually small to medium-sized businesses) who are contemplating the acquisition of a small computer are generally either using:

1.   A visible records computer.

2.   A computer bureau, or
3.   A manual system.

The major problem that they face is where to get specialised, unbiased information on how to acquire a small computer.

They require something that is cheap, matches their needs exactly and is simple to use. Such perfection is impossible and recognition of this fact represents one of the first major hurdles. (This was observed in several case studies during the project.) The choice of a machine is made more difficult by the fact that many desk-top computers have become more powerful than minicomputers.

. Decisions about the choice of computers have to be made by taking a systems view. In other words, potential users should think in terms of creating a system comprising hardware and software in their particular environment to solve specified task(s) rather than acquiring a particular machine and trying to adapt the software and/or the environment. This procedure can be facilitated by asking questions of the following type:

1.   What sort of task is to be performed?
2.   Are two tasks to be performed simultaneously?
3.   Are two or more operators to use the computer simultaneously?

One of the major problems facing users of small computers is the availability of software. Generally, professional staff and businessmen do not have the time to program computers. With large computers, the choice of a computer system is normally hardware oriented, with software being supplied to tailor the machine to the user's needs. The cost of providing this service which includes using systems analysts and programmers is very high, often running into hundreds of thousands of pounds. However, taken in the context of the cost of the hardware, it is generally acceptable.

For small computers, software must be cheap. Typical users are unlikely to tolerate software that costs in excess of 50-100 per cent of the hardware cost. (This view was supported by evidence from case studies.) Generally, this restriction precludes the use of customised software and places a reliance on packaged software and places a reliance on packaged software with installation procedures that vary with the flexibility of the package. Although this approach has the advantage of spreading the considerable cost of software development over many users, there is a danger that users will be starved of systems analysis advice (i.e. the advice that matches humans, tasks and machines). There is a tendency for purveyors of small computers to be machine-orientated and to omit the vital systems analysis role due to pressure on profit margins. To some extent, the profession of systems analysts has contributed to this situation by initially opposing the use of small computers. They have taken the view of EDP departments, activated by fears of computer anarchy (see above). Certainly there is a great need for systems analysis at the small computer level which is not being properly met.

Interestingly, however, large organisations purchase a significant number of microcomputers, implying that users in large businesses are buying microcomputers to fill a need which has not been provided for by their systems analysts.

2

Computer auditing in the small business environment: concepts and issues

INTRODUCTION

Essentially, there are two types of auditing undertaken by the profession. These are as follows:

1. Auditing for true and fair purposes.
2. Value for money auditing, and other auditing.

True and fair auditing includes statutory audits required by company law and audits of public bodies. Value for money auditing is an area which is becoming increasingly popular but is generally undertaken only by large accountancy firms mainly for public bodies such as local councils. Other auditing comprises a miscellany of jobs, such as audits of residents associations, clubs and partnerships.

   This section is concerned primarily with the impact of the computer on statutory audits of small companies, on the assumption that the smaller practices do not audit a significant number of large clients.

Conventional approaches to computer auditing

Chambers (1981) outlines the following alternative approaches to computer auditing:

1. The vouching approach which involves the ticking and checking of transaction documents to ensure that they have been correctly processed. With this approach the auditor avoids an investigation of

the computer system and relies upon the audit trail, to 'audit around' the computer system.

2. The verification approach which involves the auditor devising an independent means of verifying the existence, ownership and valuation of assets and other balance sheet, income and expenditure items.

3. The systems approach which entails an appraisal of the control features of a system in order to determine the extent to which the objectives of the system have been achieved.

Normally, auditing will involve some combination of all three techniques, though it is fair to say, as evidence from case studies and practitioners' opinions shows, that auditing for small businesses by the smaller accounting firm will usually concentrate on vouching and verification.

However, the above approaches do not specifically address themselves to the small firm environment and the following alternative framework seeks to redress this.

ALTERNATIVE APPROACHES

There are, in theory and practice, a large number of possible approaches to the audit of a computerised small business system. The rationale for a small practice to consider such an audit is that the auditor who does not adapt to the new technology, may prevent a client from making cost savings (including possible reduced external accountancy charges) which can justifiably be expected from acquiring and using the computer sensibly. The alternatives are based on evidence from the literature, empirical observation (from case studies as discussed in Chapter 6) and the opinions of practitioners (gained during the project). They include:

1. A practice approaches the audit of a small business system by 'auditing around the computer'.

2. A practice may qualify the audit of a small computerised business system, rather than becoming involved in the small business machine.

3. A practice may attempt to carry out a systems-based audit.

4. A more radical approach may be adopted, of changing the auditing requirement of a small business. For example, instead of an 'audit', a lower level of certification may be given such as a 'review' (which had a certain currency growing out of Canadian experience and supported by Gemmell (1977) and Davison (1979).

5. A novel approach is for the practice to offer what is essentially an

electronic data processing bureau service and undertake the processing of the firm's clients' accounts.

6. A practice may reprocess the complete transaction files generated by the client's system.

Each of these approaches is now discussed and analysed.

Alternative approach 1: Auditing around the computer

Auditing around a computer allows the auditor to infer the quality of the processing being carried out by *only* examining the input and output for the applications. In so doing, the auditor regards the computer as a 'black box'. But to rely on that 'black box', the auditor must also express an audit opinion of the internal control system around (and in) the computer system.

Using this approach, the firm would therefore continue to carry out vouching and would mainly perform extended manual substantive tests. However, as we will show, some doubt has been cast on its adequacy.

Arguments for auditing around the computer

There are some powerful reasons, advocated by small and large accounting firms in discussions with the Profession, for the smaller practice to continue to ignore the computer and audit around the system.

First, the advantage of auditing around the computer is simplicity and the proximity to manual auditing methods. Auditors with little technical knowledge of computer systems can be trained to perform the audit.

Second, the small practitioner does not at the moment have the ability to do otherwise. However, some firms that already employ computer specialists have made an active decision to continue auditing around the computer. The reasons why one practice chose to audit around the computer (despite having specialist computer staff), are shown in Exhibit 2.1.

Third, even if the ability and technical expertise was present in a small practice, the cost of such an audit could not be justified. The practice mentioned in the preceding paragraph chose not to carry out auditing through the computer primarily for cost reasons – though the other factors mentioned in Exhibit 2.1 were also instrumental.

Thus the cost effectiveness of auditing through the computer is in question. Cost effectiveness can be broken down into two segments:

1. The firm that chooses to audit around the computer despite specialist knowledge may do so because only relatively expensive staff have the necessary knowledge. Cheaper staff involved on vouching duties tend not to be competent to undertake a systems based audit.
2. Irrespective of the cost or availability of staff with the necessary knowledge, there is a fixed cost in a systems based audit.

Exhibit 2.1

Notes on why one practice audits around the computer

1. The practice finds that there is no cumulative detailed information maintained on microcomputers. For example, information for several years is not retained for specific accounts. In practice this has to be collected from many different pieces of computer print-out.

2. Reinforcing point 1, this practice feels that it is not possible to do a systems based audit on a microcomputer as the integrity control and disciplines concerning the microcomputer are poor or non-existent.

3. They find it difficult to use test data on a microcomputer but would be happy to do a small amount of substantive testing using a computer auditing package, if this could be done in a cost effective way.

4. Very often the practice gives a small audit certificate on the grounds that many controls which would be relevant for the large enterprise are not practical, appropriate or necessary in the small proprietary company.

5. Rather than improving internal control, microcomputers often make it worse because:
    (a) The accounting software is very poor:
    (b) It was written by a computer programmer with little under-standing of basic bookkeeping requirements.
    (c) It does not look like a book of accounts and the program does not work like a manual accounting system. Since the logic is not there, the audit trail is not there either.
    (d) The descriptions of accounts, transactions and other figures are often difficult to find. It is also not possible to find the relevant entries which make up a specific account total.

6. Often one finds a micro surrounded by a mess and this mess may be deliberately created to cover up larger sins.

Auditing through the computer requires a certain cost in documenting the system. (A suggested method is discussed later.) It involves large costs which do not vary in proportion to the number of transactions, notably the costs of documenting and reviewing the system and the cost of compliance testing in a systems based audit. In comparison, auditing around the system requires an examination of the original transactions and does not incur these costs.

Auditing around the computer will be cheaper unless these cost disadvantages are offset by savings on the cost of verification and substantive testing; and this effect is unlikely for the smallest firms.

Arguments to support the contention that systems based auditing costs are falling can be found. For example, the costs of documenting and reviewing the system and then testing it for compliance are falling as computer knowledge increases and with the greater standardisation of small business systems. On the other hand, the cost of vouching each transaction is rising as technical costs rise. Moreover some audit work can be performed using routines from clients' existing software (though this raises independence problems) and does not require special software written for the auditor.

There is some evidence to suppose that over time, the breakeven point in terms of number of transactions will become smaller and, as will be discussed in Chapter 4, the cost of documenting, review, and compliance testing may fall substantially and thereby further emphasise the cost effectiveness of a systems based audit.

Irrespective of cost, other factors should be considered in deciding whether a practice should either audit through the computer or should have some knowledge of the 'black box' (i.e. the computer) in an 'auditing around the computer' context.

Should the practitioner ignore the computer?
Why should practitioners in small practices not continue to audit around the computer? Why should they not continue to regard the data as a black box and carry out a combination of vouching and verification?

The attitude of 'ignore the computer' was found in our empirical case study work as the most widespread method of tackling the audit of a computerised small business. This section looks at why the practitioner may be advised not to rely on this solution as a pragmatic way of dealing with the new technology.

One source (Canadian Institute of Chartered Accountants, 1975) mentions five reasons why a computer environment should affect the audit approach and procedures. They are:

1. System complexities – computers with their operational speed make it possible to design systems which can carry out complex processing of large quantities of data.
2. Centralisation – all the data and information may be centralised in one system and one set of files.
3. Computer controls – computer processing demands a greater degree of control for computer systems than for other processing methods. Such controls are necessary since a computer cannot process data or react properly to situations for which adequate instructions are not available.

4. Hardware and its internal handling of information in the form of electronic impulses is inherently very reliable.
5. The electronic recording and transmission of data means that it is not visible. There are several problems arising from this:

    *   loss of visible evidence (LOVE) i.e. no documentation.
    *   loss of audit trail.

    Many of the intermediate 'hard copy' documents which could provide a visible trail from input to output may not be present in a computer system.

Within the small business context and the small practice, the auditor cannot afford to ignore the computer, for the reason that a computer system may alter the accounting system, the office environment, office procedures and so on.

To be able to audit around the computer, the auditor must be able to examine:

*   The transactions.
*   The evidence of what has happened to the transactions (i.e. an audit trail and evidence of processing).
*   The information stored by the accounting system.
*   The output produced by the system.

Most microcomputer based systems are on-line so the rationale for printing 'hard copies' of information stored in the computer is reduced. Hence it may not be possible to audit strictly around the computer. Some interaction with the computer may be necessary to produce the information necessary for an audit around the system.

If a client's software is insufficient for an audit around the computer, reprocessing of the original data (including re-coding and re-entry of original data if to be processed on a computer) may become necessary and there is a corresponding charge to the client for the accountancy work.

One other authoritative study issued by the Bank Administration Institute (1981) is concerned with small computer systems in a banking environment. Nevertheless their conclusions about the exposure to loss relate to all businesses. A list of exposure risks is shown in Table 2.1. As a computer is introduced so a business will become dependent on a system to carry out required tasks.

If the software is poor then no reliance can be placed on the 'black box' (i.e. the computer). In the event of a problem occurring inside the 'black box' the auditor will be at a loss to know what to do and is simply left with the alternative of re-performing those transactions erroneously processed.

Weber (1982) also identifies two further qualifications:

1. The type of [microcomputer] system should be limited, with no complexities in terms of size or type of processing. Yet often small business systems adopt the most sophisticated approaches.
2. The auditor cannot assess the likelihood of the system degrading if the environment changes*.

Table 2.1 Exposure to loss of a computerised system.

Interruption of operations caused by:
- dependence on computer processing
- computer failure
- loss of programs or data
- loss of key personnel

Inaccurate, unauthorised or incomplete processing owing to:
- unauthorised computer activity
- transaction errors or data manipulations
- incomplete or late processing
- disclosure of sensitive information

Unauditable systems due to:
- no permanent record of activity
- unauditable transaction journals
- incomplete identification of transactions

Loss of assets:
- fire, flood and other disasters
- destruction of the system

One further problem in relation to auditing around the computer is that the accountant will appear less knowledgeable about computer systems than the owner or employees of the client. In the event of a problem occurring inside the 'black box', the accountant will have no knowledge to be able to deal with it and must rely on manual reperformance of the transactions.

For auditing around the computer to work, we believe that a necessary condition is that the computer system should be reliable and robust with good transaction listings and reports. A small practice that is going to

---

*The system can be designed so that a change in the environment will not cause it to process data incorrectly or for it to degrade.

concentrate on auditing around the computer should therefore have the necessary expertise to judge whether the software is good or not. Better understanding of computers is a necessary pre-requisite for the continuation of auditing around the computer. Assuming that the small practitioner's knowledge does not change and that the software in the system is good, then auditing around the computer may still be a solution. However, Weber (1982) argues that auditors with little technical knowledge of computers should be managed by a computer audit specialist. This is necessary so that the robustness of the computer system and the internal controls surrounding the computer system can be reviewed. Again if a practice has insufficient knowledge, consideration can be given to the referral or sub-contracting of the work. It may not be necessary to do this annually and in some cases the review process may be carried out in three-year cycles at the discretion of the auditors.

Lack of uniformity
During the course of the project it became apparent that the practice of auditing around the computer and the resulting exposure to risk was not uniform.

In observing the type of auditing being carried out in various case studies, we noted clear distinctions in the approaches adopted and the behaviour of different firms.

For example, one firm had a good knowledge of computers but the practice decided that it could not justify auditing through the computer on cost grounds. The cost of setting up the relevant systems based audit devices would take more time than to perform a manual audit around the computer for the small number of transactions involved.

Another practice ignored the computer because of insufficient computing knowledge. In some instances, the auditors pretended to understand what the computer did. However, on further examination and questioning, it was apparent that they had little understanding of the functions performed by the computer on the data and how the programs produced the information that was sought. Exhibit 2.2 provides evidence of the type of problem.

Whilst the approach adopted in Exhibit 2.2 seeks to ensure that individual debtors are not overstated, it does not prove very useful for checking whether debts have been misallocated to individual debtors or debtors are understated. Directional testing could help in this respect, for example, by testing that goods despatched are invoiced, but this may require an examination of the internal processing undertaken by the computer.

Exhibit 2.2

A case study on the current attitude of some small to medium sized practices

The group being audited comprised 11 companies run and controlled by an entrepreneur. Each company had slightly different shareholders (usually different members of his immediate family). The turnover for the group was approximately £8m and the profit about £0.5m. The auditors were a small practice operating in the Midlands. The audit team consisted of a partner (one of about 5), a manager, one or two trainees but mainly older personnel who would be described as 'clerical' with no aspirations of becoming professionally qualified.

A minicomputer was installed by the client and the auditors adopted an around the computer approach. The only internal control in the computer system that they asked about concerned the re-payment of excess tax deducted under the PAYE procedures in the payroll suite of programs. Although a certain amount of vouching was undertaken, the real audit was balance sheet based. For this the auditors relied on computer generated reports without any knowledge of the system or the accuracy of what was produced. A debtors circularisation list was produced from the computer print-out and even though the number and the individual debtors had changed substantially since the last audit, no attempt was made to reconcile or verify the changes. (The amount of debtors outstanding could not have been dismissed as being immaterial.)

Minimal requirements

In order for auditing around the computer to remain satisfactory there are two minimal requirements: good software and some specialist computer knowledge (to ascertain the standard of the software).

Software that is amenable to auditing around the computer (with some degree of ease) may follow some of the guidelines as set out in Exhibit 2.3. We have already made a case for it to become a necessary pre-requisite for this type of auditing. Let us, however, summarise the arguments:

Exhibit 2.3

Guidelines for good software that is amenable to auditing around the computer

1. The system should be simple and batch-oriented with simple data structures and files.
2. The system should use packaged programs that are well-tested and used widely by many installations.
3. There should be a clear audit trail and detailed reports should be prepared at many processing points within the system.
4. All inputs to the system and file changes should be logged.
5. To guard against software contamination it should be difficult for there to be unauthorised modification of the package.

Good software can facilitate auditing around the computer by allowing the auditor to:

1. Place reliance on the accuracy of processing.
2. Have a degree of confidence in the accuracy and completeness of the 'transformed input' being represented by the output.
3. Collect ample evidence from computer printouts (i.e. the output) to facilitate the auditing process.

Even so, good software is not always sufficient.

Auditing around the computer: conclusion
To place reliance on an audit using this technique, we are of the opinion that good software and some specialist computer knowledge are necessary. This may not be feasible for the small practice.

For example, when a client is thinking of computerising or when a new client joins a practice with a small business system, an appraisal of that software must be carried out. If the firm has insufficient technical expertise then one of several actions could be followed:

1. The work can be referred to another accounting firm with the necessary knowledge.
2. The work can be sub-contracted to a computer company/software house with the necessary ability. (This option is discussed in a later section.)

It is our belief that the software should be reviewed periodically if reliance is to be placed on auditing around the system.

Alternative approach 2: Small audit qualifications
Small businesses may require qualification. Exhibit 2.4 shows an example of such a qualification. Exhibit 2.5 contains a more strongly-worded example. Both qualifications related to actual case studies of computer based accounting systems.

There are two instances where such an approach may be relevant:

1. A practice may start to use this qualification due to the acquisition of a computer by its client.
2. A practice may already be using this approach prior to the computerisation of its client, the advent of a computer making little difference to the approach and in fact adding further justification to it.

The use of such a qualification varies. From the case studies, it was

Exhibit 2.4

Small business audit qualification

We have audited the financial statements on pages XXX in accordance with approved auditing standards.

In common with many businesses of a similar size and organisation the Company's system of control is dependent upon the close involvement of the directors (who are major shareholders). Where independent confirmation of the completeness of the accounting records was not available, we have accepted assurances from the directors that all the company's transactions have been reflected in the records.

Subject to the foregoing, in our opinion the financial statements, which have been prepared under the historical cost convention give a true and fair view of the state of the company's affairs at [date] and of its result and source and application of funds for the year then ended and comply with the Companies Acts 1948 to 1981, insofar as the provisions of those Acts apply to these financial statements.

Exhibit 2.5

A stronger small business audit qualification

During the period under review internal control over management has been limited, as is the case with many other businesses of similar size and organisation. There have been no practical audit procedures to determine the effect of this limitation.

Stock has been valued by the directors and we are unable to form an opinion upon the accuracy of this figure. Consequently heavy reliance has been placed upon the representations of management. It would appear that proper accounting records, as strictly required by the Companies Act 1976, have not been kept.

Subject to the above, in our opinion, the annexed Balance Sheet, Profit and Loss Account and Notes, which have been prepared on the historical cost basis of accounting, give on this basis a true and fair view of the state of the company's affairs as at 30 June 1983, and of the loss and source and application of funds for the year ended on that date, and comply with the Companies Acts 1948 to 1981.

apparent that some firms qualify up to 90 per cent of their clients whilst others hardly ever use the qualification – even though, in our opinion, they would be justified in using it. This diversity of convention is a disturbing feature in itself.

In the case studies, we detected a tendency for a greater use of the small audit qualification where a small business system was involved.

Interestingly, in his research report to the ICAEW, Page (1981) found that from a random sample of 400 small companies only 2 per cent were qualified by their auditors on the grounds of 'insufficient internal control to express an opinion' and 94 per cent received 'clean' audit reports. This research finding presumably refers to a more serious deficiency than that dealt with in Exhibit 2.5. Although these two findings might suggest an inconsistency, Page's evidence concerned situations in which there was insufficient internal control to *express* an opinion while Exhibits 2.4 and 2.5 are an opinion, albeit a qualified one.

As an effective way to deal with the problem, the profession may wish to extend and expand the scope of the small audit qualification especially to cater for small business systems.

Alternative approach 3: Systems-based audit

The third approach is to carry out a systems-based audit.

According to Jenkins and Pinkney (1980), the difference between a computer and a non-computer audit is as follows:

> The audit approach in a computer system is similar to that in a non-computer system. The auditor should understand and record the accounting system, evaluate the system of internal controls and carry out functional (sometimes known as compliance) tests to satisfy himself that the controls are working in practice. In so doing, the auditor will have to evaluate and test new forms of control and to use new techniques.

The approach as defined here is very much a systems based approach. What this entails is discussed more fully in Chapter 3. There are two problems for the small practice. First the small practice may be in no position:

1. To understand and record the accounting system if it is based on new technology.
2. To evaluate the system of internal control since
    (a) the practitioner may not be aware of what constitutes good internal control, and
    (b) small businesses have always been the subject of doubtful control before the new technology.
3. To carry out compliance tests since the practitioner in this event does not understand the system and does not know what constitutes good control and is even in less of a position to test that control.

This places a great burden of identifying and placing reliance on the internal controls. A separate chapter (Chapter 4), is therefore devoted to internal controls.

There are two possible approaches to the systems-based audit of a small business system:

1. Adopt the conventional or perceived computer auditing approach.
2. Develop a new approach more relevant to the needs and controls of a small business.

These are outlined in greater detail in Chapter 3.

Second, if a firm is to attempt a systems-based audit, a higher standard of computer knowledge is required than we believe is necessary for auditing around computers. This ability will include both technical knowledge of computer systems, and technical ability to use a computer as a tool and to use it advantageously from the auditing point of view. (Note that the technical knowledge of computers required in this case is much greater than the lower level that we have suggested is necessary for auditing around the computer.)

In order to acquire such knowledge the small practice takes one of several courses of action:

(a) The purchase of the services of an expert in computer audit work. Such a person would cost over £16000 plus overheads in 1985. In the future some graduates who have specialised in computerised accountancy at university or polytechnic may represent a cheaper short-run solution.
(b) One of the professional staff could start to acquire the necessary knowledge of computers.
(c) The work could be sub-contracted to a computer company or software house or referred to a larger practice with the necessary expertise.

All three methods of gaining the necessary expertise have been adopted in the UK and US. However there is some evidence in the UK and to a greater extent in the US to put forward the disturbing hypothesis: that some smaller firms may attempt to learn systems based auditing 'on the job' and pretend to knowledge which they do not have. We found some evidence of this in our case studies.

If these examples are not isolated (and we do not believe that they are) then the evidence is disturbing for the Profession. There are three implications. First the objectives of the audit may not be achieved. Second the trust placed in the Profession's hands might be betrayed. Third such behaviour would be inconsistent with that trust and the traditional role and image of the Profession.

As will be pointed out in Chapter 4, it is still very difficult to carry out a proper systems based audit in computerised small businesses. Later we identify some new solutions, but they must be coupled with an investment in specialist computer staff or the ability to refer work. Many firms, however, will have too small a client base to justify the need for expensive specialists.

Alternative approach 4: Change auditing requirements for a small business
The Profession has already considered whether current audit requirements are practical and sensible for small companies or whether a less strict requirement of 'reviewing' the records of a client should be adopted.

In practical terms, many of the smaller practices encountered during the project were already implementing a form of review. This was being achieved in two ways:

1. The increasing use of the small audit qualification irrespective of whether or not it is justified (as in Alternative approach 2).
2. A re-interpretation or lowering of auditing standards, thereby making a two tier level of standards.

The difference between these two approaches is that extending the small audit qualification is a minor variation of the existing practice. A 'review' or some similar concept would be a major departure from the current practice in the UK.

In West Germany, the second method has been adopted; there is a sharp distinction between the 'Wirtshaftsprufer' who only audit the largest firms, and the 'Steuerberater' who do the rest.

The justification for fundamentally re-thinking whether or not small businesses should be audited is a realisation that many internal control concepts such as separation of duties are inapplicable. Even some of the newer internal control solutions are fraught with problems; owner-directors who have some computer expertise are still liable to create errors and/or misrepresent the state of the business. It may be argued that because it is normally impossible to carry out a proper audit of a small company, the Profession should remove the requirement.

If the requirement were removed this could improve the credibility of the Profession with the public. There is some possibility that Parliament may legislate before the Profession deals with this question. The current Conservative government has examined ways of reducing the paperwork and regulation of small businesses (*viz* the enterprise zones and registration requirements) and a future strategy may consist of examining the auditing requirements. It may be better for the Profession to seek reforms of its own volition, rather than have them externally imposed.

One objection might be the loss of business represented by 'audit' fees from small clients. There are two replies to this objection. First, the problem is not too serious for the very small practice – the number of audits carried out are strictly limited, most of the fees being gained through tax, accounting and secretarial work. For the larger practice (although small to medium in absolute terms) audit fees may be a more significant proportion but it will still not form the majority of the fee income of the practice. This may not be true of some medium size practices.

However, the loss of audit income may be replaced by two types of new sources of fee income:

1. The review fees could almost compensate for the loss of audit income.
2. We believe that new sources of fee income could more than replace the difference between the review and the audit fee. These new services might include that offered in alternative approach 5 (a bureau service), and advice on computerising a client's accounts and other types of managerial help, advice and service. For example, as well as helping with computing advice, an accounting practice could offer personnel selection help and advice (similar to some large firms but on a small local scale), advice and help on loans including the negotiation of loans (a service equivalent to mortgage brokers for house buyers), advice on insurance (already performed by many practices), and many other 'managerial' services. The scope and type of review work could be varied with the nature and size of the company.

In fact, this increase in the range of services could improve the image of the accountant, and the help he may give to his clients. However, many of these services are already given to audit clients notwithstanding the supposed ethical problems of so doing. By making it legitimate to offer these services, this course of action would extend these services.

One other course of action may be considered appropriate for the Government to take. Many small companies were set up as legitimate tax avoidance schemes. One way of reducing the numbers of these companies would be for the Government to declare an amnesty for the shareholders of these companies to switch their assets to some form of partnership without a tax penalty. This, in effect, would reduce the number of audits to be performed and could be coupled with some form of review process for partnership work. This may increase fee income as partnerships are not 'reviewed' at the moment and some partnerships with less adequate records may ask accounting firms to carry out the preparation of these records.

However, the proposal to change the audit requirement to a 'review' requirement has some disadvantages. Difficulty may be found in defining the scope of reviews. Firms may be forced to limit their work to the point at which errors are not discovered and then, indeed, may find themselves being sued for negligent 'review'.

Alternative approach 5: Offer a bureau service

A further approach to solving the problem of the small business system was for the firm to offer a bureau type service for its clients.

In doing work themselves, accounting firms obviously run into an ethical problem. However, some practices feel strongly that this is a sensible and logical way to proceed, since:

1. Auditing on microcomputers is fraught with difficulties as many controls and disciplines surrounding the computer are poor or non-existent.
2. Software on a microcomputer is often poor with insufficient accounting information and no audit trail or logging of data.
3. The microcomputer can be surrounded by poor office procedures resulting in what can only be described as a 'mess'.

The advantages to be gained from offering such a data processing service include:

1. Good disciplines and procedures can be imposed on the client prior to computer processing.
2. By doing the routine data processing work, the accounting firm performs some of the preliminary work for the preparation and audit of the year end accounts. This has several advantages:
   (a) The preparation of accounts is carried out to a high standard.
   (b) The internal control surrounding the computer can also be of a high standard. The audit procedure can concentrate on the accuracy and completeness of the information being prepared for processing. Maintenance of data can be performed on the basis of reminding the client to review standing data.
   (c) By undertaking this work for a number of clients the accounting practice can gain economies of scale which would not be available to each client operating in isolation.

It should be noted that we are not proposing a split of work for bureau service (e.g. invoicing from sales ledger maintenance). Such a split would prevent automatic ledger posting integrated with invoice production.

This approach assumes that the practice would undertake all the data processing needs, including invoicing and their mailing.

If a bureau service is offered, then an accounting firm should pay attention to offering clients a comprehensive service with carefully designed forms, good control procedures, and a variety of reports providing good management information. There will be an automatic separation of duties in that the client (the initiator and authoriser of data) is distinct from the person recording and processing the data. A partner or suitably-qualified person could, if necessary, review the data input and processing. A management accounting/budgetary control service could also be offered as an 'additional extra'.

Typically, bureau work begins with payroll work and extends into general and subsidiary ledger work and the operation of a management accounting system.

In many ways, apart from the ethical problems, this is a most satisfactory solution. The small business does not have to become too involved in technology which is not properly understood, nor adopt office procedures that are at best considered a necessary evil. However, the accounting practice will have to know and understand its own computer system. Knowledge of one system may be easier to learn than a general knowledge of computers. This type of service can be cost effective for the client. For the accounting firm, it can be a method of spreading the fixed costs of operating a computer which is used to run the practice administration and from case studies it is evident that some practices are already making a useful additional contribution to net fees from running such a service.

Alternative approach 6: Reprocessing the complete transaction files generated by the client's system

This approach is based on an events accounting system which is discussed further in Chapter 4. It differs from Approach 5 in that the client's software would also produce an events or transactions file which could be read and reprocessed on a practice's computer. Basically each economic event or transaction is stored by the system together with all the necessary information relating to that transaction. If clients were urged to adopt such a system whereby events were stored in a standard file format, the auditor could copy these files to his or her machine (perhaps on a floppy disc).

For such systems, a processing or reprocessing of a vouched transaction file for the period, by an independent program on an independent machine, under controlled conditions will provide the auditor with much of the processing evidence he needs without substantial audit cost or inconvenience to the client.

This alternative is another acceptable way forward through the morass surrounding systems audits, and is particularly applicable to computer based accounting systems in small firms. This alternative differs from the 'bureau service' option of 'Alternative 5', in that it:

1. Leaves with the client the responsibility for creating the data file at the times and places he wishes.
2. Leaves the labour intensive jobs of initial coding of transactions and of data entry to the client.
3. Leaves the client free to do anything or nothing with the data on the transaction file, as the client may choose for himself, without raising questions about the auditable quality of subsequent processing adopted by the client.
5. Is free from some of the ethical problems that may surround bureau operation.
5. May be less expensive or inconvenient to the client.

All that is required for the approach to be adopted is that the auditor should have a program he regards as adequate for producing reports he wants from client data, and transaction files in a known format prepared by his client, in a form readable by the auditor's machine (presumably from a compatible disc or through a network).

CONCLUSION

Having introduced these six alternative approaches, the next two chapters introduce the concepts of a systems based audit and internal controls within a computer based environment. They are considered an introductory guide to factors which need to be considered when working with computers.

3

Computer audit approaches and techniques

INTRODUCTION

A systems-based audit can be carried out in a computerised or non-computerised system.

There are many different methods of conducting audits and the advent of a computer adds extra dimensions to each of these methods. A general description of a systems based audit is described below. This can be compared with the general approach to a conventional audit (see, for example, De Paula and Attwood, 1982).

Step 1: Understanding and recording the system
This involves the flowcharting (see Figure 3.1) and description (usually by narrative notes of various operations in the flowchart) of both the parts of the system performed by the computer and those parts performed manually. For example, sales orders may be raised manually but invoices may be prepared by the computer. Both operations must be recorded systematically.

The length of time taken to perform this intricate task is often underestimated. As such it represents a fixed cost in that it has to be carried out irrespective of the number of transactions or size of the business. As well as flowcharting, it will involve system descriptions, walk-throughs and so on. (See Weber, 1982 or Jenkins and Pinkney, 1980).

Step 2: Evaluation of internal controls
Exactly what is meant by internal controls is discussed more fully in Chapter 4. Two examples are given for a computer system in which

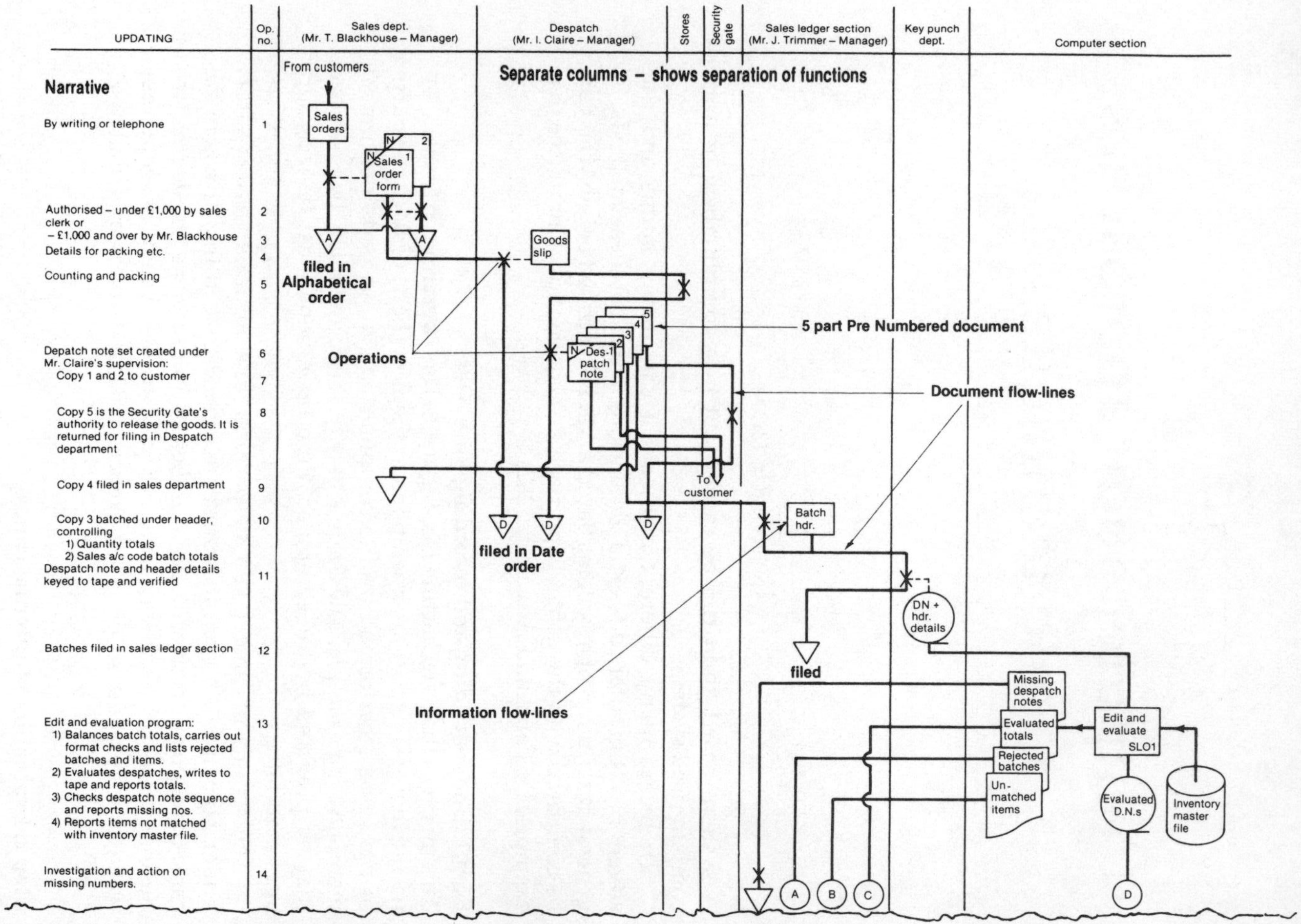
UPDATING
Op. no.
Sales dept. (Mr. T. Blackhouse – Manager)
Despatch (Mr. I. Claire – Manager)
Stores
Security gate
Sales ledger section (Mr. J. Trimmer – Manager)
Key punch dept.
Computer section
Narrative
From customers
Separate columns – shows separation of functions
By writing or telephone
1
Sales orders
Sales order form
Authorised – under £1,000 by sales clerk or
2
– £1,000 and over by Mr. Blackhouse
3
Details for packing etc.
4
Goods slip
filed in Alphabetical order
Counting and packing
5
5 part Pre Numbered document
Depatch note set created under Mr. Claire's supervision:
6
Copy 1 and 2 to customer
7
Operations
Des-patch note
Document flow-lines
Copy 5 is the Security Gate's authority to release the goods. It is returned for filing in Despatch department
8
Copy 4 filed in sales department
9
To customer
Copy 3 batched under header, controlling
10
1) Quantity totals
2) Sales a/c code batch totals
Batch hdr.
Despatch note and header details keyed to tape and verified
11
filed in Date order
DN + hdr. details
Batches filed in sales ledger section
12
filed
Missing despatch notes
Information flow-lines
Edit and evaluation program:
13
1) Balances batch totals, carries out format checks and lists rejected batches and items.
2) Evaluates despatches, writes to tape and reports totals.
3) Checks despatch note sequence and reports missing nos.
4) Reports items not matched with inventory master file.
Evaluated totals
Edit and evaluate SLO1
Rejected batches
Un-matched items
Evaluated D.N.s
Inventory master file
Investigation and action on missing numbers.
14

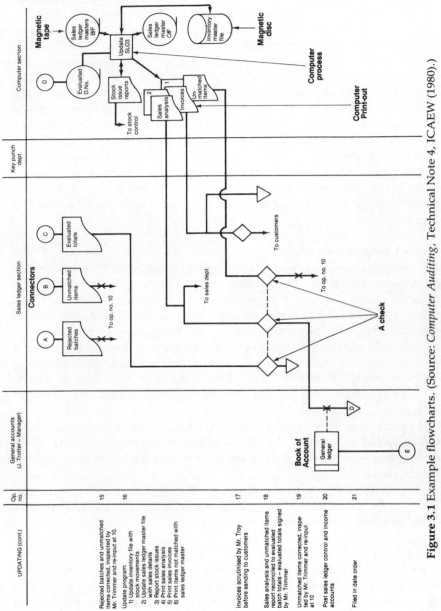

Figure 3.1 Example flowcharts. (Source: *Computer Auditing*, Technical Note 4, ICAEW (1980).)

invoices are raised manually and then input in batches to a computer system. If the invoices are pre-numbered and use a sequential numbering system, the computer can perform a 'sequence check' to ensure that all the invoice numbers are in sequence; missing invoices or other invoices out of sequence can be reported on for appropriate action. Similarly a pre-list total of the invoice value can be input separately as a batch total of the value of invoices; the computer can then record a running total of the invoices as they are input. At the end, the batch total and the running total can be compared and the user warned if the two disagree. The sequence check is an example of an internal control concerned with ensuring that all invoices are input whereas the batch total ensures that all invoices are input *correctly*. In so far as the sequence of input is concerned with the completeness of input of all invoices, a batch total will govern both the completeness and accuracy of input. This theme will be returned to in Chapter 4.

Step 3: Compliance testing

If the controls are strong enough, compliance tests should be performed on those controls which the auditor wishes to rely on. For example, the sequence check deals with completeness of input but the batch total check covers accuracy of input as well as completeness. The auditor could therefore rely on the batch total and discard the sequence check.

Normally compliance tests and the evaluation of internal controls are noted on one form, sometimes called the internal control questionnaire or internal control evaluation form. The compliance tests follow similar procedures to those in a manual system. Table 3.1 shows an example of such a form with specimen compliance tests.

In particular, with a control such as a batch control, the compliance testing would ensure that the check was working and that there was a manual follow-up of any discrepancies between the batch total and the running total.

At the end of Step 3, a record of control weaknesses will be made and those to be recorded in the management letter (or internal control memorandum) are noted.

Step 4: Substantive testing

Some substantive tests (sometimes known as validation procedures) will be necessary whatever happens at Stage 3. If the controls are weak or if the compliance tests on the controls show that they are not operating properly, then the nature and extent of the substantive tests will be increased.

Table 3.1 Internal control evaluation

Key Control Question	Evaluation	FC Ref. Yes/No	Compliance tests		Comments Letter Points		Substantive tests
	Principal controls (nature and effect of weaknesses)		Description	Results	Yes/No	Ref.	Nature and extent
Can goods be despatched without being charged to a customer? Controls over computer processing To be completed where details of goods despatched are input to the computer and updated after pricing to the sales ledger masterfile. By reference to the control cards, identify the principal control and answer the computer questions for each of the control requirements listed under I.A. below.	1. Controls over computer processing A.1. Completeness of Input Computer sequence check of serially numbered despatch notes.	13.3 √	• Test by observation and examination that all despatches are recorded on serially numbered despatch notes. • Examine missing despatch note report for evidence that missing items are regularly reported and that duplicate items are rejected. • Examine missing despatch note report for evidence that reported items are being dealt with. • Verify that there is no undue volume or value of uncleared items. • Select a sample of reported despatch note numbers and ensure that these have been adequately investigated and corrected.				

Source: *Computer Auditing*, ICAEW (1980)

The computer, by means of computer assisted audit techniques (CAAT), can aid the substantive testing process through the validation and extraction of information from the computerised records (see Appendix 3 for a brief overview of CAATS). For example, on a computerised stock file where details of the date when a stock count was taken, the computer could be made to list all stock items (and their associated value) which did not have a physical stock count during the year. Such computer audit interrogation software, as it is known, can be very powerful. We will return to the use of CAATs later in the chapter.

The importance of internal controls on which the auditor can place reliance must be emphasised. For example a batch total check must not only be seen to be working, but the auditor must make sure that no-one has contaminated the software (i.e. altered the software so that it looks as if the control is working although the computer has not performed the check).

Readers interested in learning more about systems-based auditing should consult Malcolm and Meadows (1983), Chambers (1981), Weber (1982), Jenkins and Pinkney (1980) and Jancura (1977) or one of the other computer auditing texts mentioned in the bibliography.

ADOPTION BY SMALL PRACTICE

Having outlined the fundamentals of a systems-based audit it is interesting to consider whether or not a small practice should carry out such an audit.

There are, however, problems for the small practice in conducting a systems-based audit. These problems were discussed in Chapter 2 but are summarised here. The first problem is that Step 1 itself involves a number of phases which represent a fixed cost in that it has to be carried out irrespective of the number of transactions or size of the business. Secondly the small practice may be in no position:

1.   To understand and record the accounting system if it is based on new technology.
2.   To evaluate the system of internal control, since
     (a) the practitioner may not be aware of what constitutes good internal control, and
     (b) small businesses have always been the subject of doubtful control before the new technology.
3.   To carry out compliance tests since the practitioner in this event does not understand the system and does not know what constitutes good control and is even in less of a position to test that control.

This places a great burden of identifying and placing reliance on the internal controls which is discussed in the next chapter.

A third problem is that if a firm is to attempt a systems- based audit, a higher standard of computer knowledge is required than we believe is necessary for auditing around computers. This knowledge is greatly increased if CAATs are to be used and this is further discussed in Appendix 3.

What can be said in favour of a systems-based audit? Obviously the knowledge and experience of computers is being increased within the profession. In time the profession will have greatly increased knowledge.

The main argument for a systems-based audit is one of efficiency or cost. More audit comfort is provided for less (or the same) cost. The counter argument is that it requires some expertise and the volume of transactions may have to be sufficiently large to justify the fixed costs of a systems-based audit. However even if an audit 'around the computer' is performed, some appraisal of the computing environment may be necessary.

The computerisation of a system changes the conditions and therefore the exposure to much of both the accounting records and the audit. The auditor must be able to understand what the computer has produced. If there is a serious loss of visible evidence, the auditor may have to reperform checks conducted by the computer.

With the increased use of microcomputers, data will be entered direct into the computer and business transactions will increasingly be paperless. This heralds a situation in which there may be no 'around the computer' environment. In this instance a systems-based audit may be mandatory as, apart from the computer itself, there is little or no evidence in support of the accounting records.

One view (see for example Robin Mathieson's paper in ICAEW, June 1983), is that auditors will require to have access to each transaction in the case of weak internal and computer controls.

If controls are not adequate and evidence as to their efficiency cannot be collected, then auditors will require access to each transaction. Access would be by means of the provision of an audit trail either printed or in magnetic form (e.g. on a floppy disc) or by the use of a piece of software, residing in the machine, which tests the efficacy (as defined by the auditor) of each transaction as it occurs and to save some for further examination whilst discarding the rest.

SHOULD A PRACTICE USE COMPUTER ASSISTED AUDIT TECHNIQUES?

Computer-assisted audit techniques (CAATS) can concentrate on a few key areas:

1. Test data: this can be achieved by means of the interactive input of certain transactions.
2. File interrogation software: there may be mainstream file interrogation packages to work under certain microprocessor based operating systems or there may be application-specific packages which are written faster but only achieve say 80 per cent of the objectives of the package.
3. Integrity control software such as source code comparison programs, program library analysers, terminal logs identifying users and recording activities undertaken.

In general (3) is less well developed than (1) or (2) and with microcomputers, there are very few general purpose file interrogation packages. See Appendix 3 for a further explanation of these terms.

Two particular problems are associated in using CAATS with microcomputers. First, the level of expertise of the auditor is usually less well-developed than it would be in a mainframe environment. Even if the work is referred to a larger accounting firm, the cost of the staff time necessary to undertake CAATS is high. The second reason is that CAATS usually require an overhead of several days or even weeks (several auditing experts familiar with the use of CAATS considered that three weeks was the shortest period in which CAATS could be implemented. For reasons already explained, this period might be reduced over time). Such an additional burden on the audit of a small business system could not be justified. We assume however that with adequate training it would be possible for many small practices to carry out a range of simple CAATS.

The APC's auditing guideline on computer assisted audit techniques referred to small computers in remarking 'Where the enterprise uses a small computer the general principles in this guideline are still appropriate'.

However, differences are mentioned and these include:

1. A greater emphasis on substantive testing may be needed when small computers are used.
2. Audit software packages may not work on small computers.
3. The smaller volumes processed by small computers may render manual methods more cost effective.

4

Internal control in the small computerised business

INTRODUCTION

In the previous chapter, the effectiveness of internal controls was a key element of a systems-based audit. This chapter first provides a brief introduction to internal controls.

There are two types of internal controls:

1. General controls surrounding the computer hardware, software and operating environment.
2. Specific controls over the computer applications.

The Institute's APC's Auditing guidelines provide a classification of general and application controls:

Application controls	General controls
Controls over input	Controls over application development
Controls over processing	Controls to prevent or detect unauthorised
Controls over master files and	changes to programs
standing data	Controls to ensure that all program changes
contained therein	are adequately tested and documented
	Controls to prevent or detect errors during
	program execution
	Controls to prevent unauthorised
	amendment to data files
	Controls to ensure that system software is
	properly installed and maintained
	Controls to ensure that proper
	documentation is kept
	Controls to ensure continuity of operations

The application controls are usually devised in order to achieve various audit objectives such as:

- Completeness of input.
- Accuracy of input.
- Authorisation.
- Completeness and accuracy of updating.
- Maintenance of data.

Examples of application controls which fall within the share audit objectives are shown in Table 4.1.

An alternative classification used by Jenkins and Pinkney (1980)

Table 4.1 Application control techniques for computer systems.

Completeness of input
Computer sequence check of serially numbered input documents
Computer matching
Agreement of manually established batch totals
Checking of print-outs of items written to the file with retained copies

Accuracy of input
Controls used for completeness of input
Edit checks in programs (e.g. check digit verification, reasonableness checks, dependency checks, existence checks and double matching)
Use of pre-recorded input (e.g. account numbers on cheques)
Scrutiny of output

Authorisation
Manual authorisation
Checking of users' passwords
Programmed authorisation of input data (e.g. comparison of balance plus transaction value to credit limit)

Completeness and accuracy of updating
Controls used for completeness of input applied after update
Manual agreement of computer established input totals
Computer agreement of computer established input totals (run to run controls)

Maintenance of data
Reconciliation of file totals
Detailed checking of data
Exception reporting
File access restrictions

Source: Malcolm and Meadows (1983)

involves a four-way classification scheme in which general controls are broadly sub-divided into integrity controls and disciplines; application controls into user controls and programmed procedures. This classification is especially useful in assessing the practicalities of internal controls within a small business environment. An explanation of these controls is given below.

1. User controls – defined as normal controls carried out on the data being processed.
2. Programmed procedures are controls embedded in a program either to replace normal controls or to carry out certain calculations of a routine nature. Any input/edit checks fall into this category.
3. Integrity controls are mainly 'general controls' under the previous nomenclature and fall into one of four purposes:
   - Implementation controls.
   - Program security controls.
   - Computer operations controls.
   - Data file security controls.
4. Disciplines over basic controls are those features which are designed to ensure that the basic controls continue to operate properly. They can be divided into supervisory duties, and custodial controls. Examples of these controls are shown in Table 4.2.

RELEVANCE OF INTERNAL CONTROLS

Given that the practitioner has the necessary expertise and ability to follow through a computer audit, the next question to be raised is the relevance and usefulness of computer controls in a small business.

User controls
User controls in a small business environment are usually weak. The basic clerical controls and disciplines do not exist and unless the controls are programmed into the software, users are unlikely to change their habits.

Programmed controls
Usually it is the adequacy of the programmed controls which becomes important. The data processing mode is often on-line data input and/or on-line and real-time file update. Data is usually entered on-line through a keyboard with a VDU by the user. The data is edited, verified and balanced on entry. The majority of data files are accessible for enquiry and direct update. The reconciliation of input control totals with computer generated totals is often not practicable.

Table 4.2

User controls
    Batch totals
    Missing or rejected items investigated
    Reviews of output/computer printout checking
    Quantity shipped checked

Programmed procedures
    Sequence check
    Calculations

Integrity controls
    Implementation
    Program security
    Computer operations
    Data file security

Disciplines
    Supervisory – supervision of investigated missing documents
    Segregation of duties – should involve the work of one person providing a
       check over the operation of another
    Custodial – separation of custody from record inquiry, physical security

Integrity controls
In general they are weak or non-existent so that little reliance can be placed on these controls.

Disciplines
Similarly, the disciplines are either weak or non-existent. For example:

- There is no supervision of the investigation of missing documents.
- There is no segregation of duties involving the work of one person providing a check over the operation of another; the checking of computer printouts may be performed by the person who entered the data.
- There are few or no custodial functions; the separation of custody of assets from record-keeping may not exist and the physical control of stock may be weak. When goods are shipped there may be no physical check and no separation of the custody function.

Consequently, reliance cannot be placed upon internal controls. This has an impact both on auditing around and through a computer.

Conventional computer auditing would necessitate reliance on:

1. General controls such as integrity controls.
2. Either satisfactory user controls and programmed procedures or sufficiently strong programmed procedures to overcome any deficiency in user controls.

If these two conditions are not present then no reliance can be placed on controls. Within a microprocessor-based system, general data processing controls over administration and systems development are often non-existent. This was confirmed by evidence from larger accounting firms and our own investigations. User controls are weak and the programmed procedures are not strong enough to be reliable.

Obviously there are many approaches to the internal control weaknesses of microcomputers. Chapter 2 explicitly looked at some of the approaches. Within the context of a systems based audit what do these control weaknesses mean? Appendix 4 examines their implications for systems based audits. Better designed hardware and software controls essentially build in the integrity controls and the use of plentiful programmed procedures ensures more complete and accurate input of data and updating.

WHAT CAN BE DONE TO IMPROVE INTERNAL CONTROLS?

The literature has concentrated on urging the development of good software in order to build in controls and to develop an audit trail. However this does not overcome the lack of general controls or indeed the lack of segregation of duties. Often a transaction will be initiated, authorised, recorded (i.e. input to the computer system) and reviewed by the same person.

What can be done to improve internal controls? There are two conflicting methodologies. One is to attempt to force the small business to adopt minimum standards of control on the grounds that small computers are no different from other computers.

The imposition of minimum standards of control would involve specialist computer staff and the segregation of duties within an accounting department.

The alternative methodological standpoint is to let the business managers (i.e. the users) use the computer as a management tool in any way they please. Management tend to ignore the traditional problem areas such as separation of duties, limited access to the system and extensive documentation. Good internal controls such as limiting access and requiring extra personnel would negate the advantages of the small computer and may be compared with the removal of direct dialling telephones and the installation of a central operator monitoring a switchboard (Cargill, 1981).

In this particular methodology, it is accepted that the environment of the small computer is fundamentally different from the environment of the large computer. There are two basic approaches:

1. The use of new and fundamentally different controls which will replace traditional internal ones.
2. The design of better hardware and software based on existing technology. In this approach the microcomputer would improve internal control and this improvement would be transparent to the user, though some good clerical procedures and disciplines would be necessary. This approach makes it easier to implement a systems based computer audit.

Both of these approaches are now discussed in more detail.

Newer and less restrictive approaches

Two simple examples of new types of control are given.

The first example concerns the convention that computers and terminals should have limited access. Cargill (1981) developed a different solution. In a small business where there may not be room, an alternative to locking away the computer and terminals is to have them in plain sight. This may deter the casual user from 'playing'.

Secondly, segregation of duties can be performed by means of software. The process of allocating functions amongst accounting and computer staff can be assisted by an appropriate choice of what functions are to be included on menus. If reliance is placed on menus to establish an allocation of functions it must be ensured that they are not changed without proper authorisation and that access to a menu requires a password. If responsibilities cannot be allocated in this way, some initial computer reports will have to be run very carefully, especially any which result in payments to employees or suppliers.

THE CARGILL AND LITECKY SOLUTION

The environment of a small computer is usually fundamentally different from the environment surrounding a large computer. The direct involvement and knowledge of the owner replace the techniques needed to ensure that management's policies are followed. An assumption is made about the integrity of the data based on the owner's direct knowledge of operations and difficulties encountered in the data processing function.

Involvement

The involvement of the owner/manager may be the most important concept in the internal control of a small firm. Management should know all the customers and suppliers, and perhaps have a fair idea of what is being purchased and at about what price. In other words, management can review the subsidiary ledgers and general ledger accounts with the auditor. Such a process represents internal control of an informal manner.

The process of reviewing and questioning management about their operations would become progressively easier following the introduction of a small computer. During the first year there would be much questioning and discussion about the accounts, customers, suppliers and employees. In subsequent years attention can be focused on the changes. The transaction details would still need to be reviewed.

There are, however, some circumstances in which involvement may not be possible. The following is a case found during our research.

Case study where involvement is not possible

The company produces consumer products using both metal and plastic covers. The turnover is around £12 million and at the moment the company is trading at a loss. Production is organised into three divisions; plastics and moulding, metal, and assembly operations. About 200 people work for the company. There is a Chairman who represents the original owners of the firm, a new director who was brought in to rescue the company, along with new and. badly-needed capital from the City. The financial director is primarily concerned with secretarial functions and day-to-day control of the cash. He has not been able to communicate with the data processing manager who is 'something of a tough guy'. Around 10,000 orders are processed weekly from a product list of thousands and there are around 10,000 raw material parts.

Although such a company may be classified as small, the volume of processing is large. Direct involvement of the routine operations is therefore impossible with the current volume. Consequently the company appointed a controller to provide supervision and review of the DP department and to improve control.

Detachment

In this type of environment it is necessary for the owner to be detached with the consequence that *either* the traditional types of controls are required *or* increased and extensive use is made of those controls now described.

Getting the computer to do the work

Earlier in this section we mentioned two conflicting methodologies: one which emphasised the restoration of the minimum standards of control and the other which retained the freedom of microcomputers but considered less restrictive approaches. One way of retaining this freedom is to achieve control through new hardware and software solutions.

HARDWARE CONFIGURATION

The types of hardware configuration which may be appropriate for small business machines can be divided into three categories:

1. Hardware solutions involving current technology.
2. Hardware solutions involving current technology plus some bespoke hardware.
3. Hardware solutions involving new technology.

Point 2 is not readily available and 3 is more futuristic; these are explored more fully in Appendix 5. The first solution is now considered.

We envisage in these circumstances a small business machine system consisting of the following:

> 2 floppy disc drives
> 1 VDU
> 1 hard disc
> 1 streamer tape drive
> 1 printer

The hard disc would contain the data files, the streamer tape drive would be used for copying and/or transaction logging, one of the floppy disc drives would be used to keep the operating system and programs, and the second floppy disc drive would log all transactions and changes to standing data.

Other features which would be useful include:

*   The provision of a battery operated or rechargeable clock. All transactions and data changes would be associated with a time read by the machine. Data would be unalterable by human intervention except for the maintenance engineer who would be able to re-set the time and date (and if necessary change the batteries).
*   The hardware and software would prohibit the compilation, editing or re-loading of any programs.
*   The system should not be capable of being run on start-up or being shut-down without security copies of the master files being taken, and appropriate action taken with the floppies. This function should

be enforced by firmware (i.e. software embedded in the hardware).

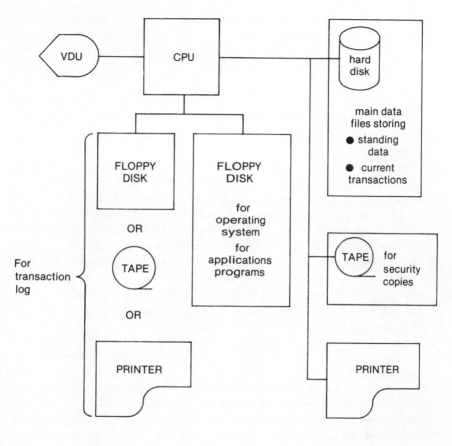

Figure 4.1

- In addition to using hardware or firmware, a record of all transactions should be kept. The data should be written on to a machine-readable device in a standardised format so that it could be read by an auditor's machine. Transactions may be coded by (a), commands and (b), input of data. The latter could be further split into (1), transactions and (2), changes to standing data. Each data input could subsequently be sub-divided into one of a number of functional areas (e.g. sales, purchases, payroll, inventory, general ledger and so on).

SOFTWARE SOLUTIONS

The principles of good control using software can be labelled 'simple software solutions' and these are summarised below. (Note that there is a partial duplication of hardware solutions; a particular operation can therefore be enforced either by hardware or by software.)

Simple software solutions:

1. A guaranteed transactions listing and audit trail, including the ability to obtain a hard copy of these.
2. Enforcing the security copying of all files at the beginning or end of the day.
3. The inability to compile or load programs. Only programs in executable code should be maintained on the system.
4. All file changes should be logged and a hard copy obtained.
5. Master file re-creation from the old master file plus the currently logged transactions and standing data changes should be possible.
6. The transaction input program should have an extensive set of editing, validity and reasonableness checks. Ideally there should be length and type checks for each field of data. For customers, suppliers and payroll, both an account number and a name may be input for an additional redundancy check. Check digit verification for an account number should be performed.
7. Transactions, once input, should not be capable of amendment. The equivalent of an amendment can only be made by two further transactions:
   (a) One cancelling the original transaction (but both are retained in the transaction listing for inspection), and
   (b) a record stating the new (and corrected) form of the transaction.
8. Menus can perform some of the segregation of duties. For example, the interrogation of files is usually lumped in with such general features as:

   insert/add
   delete
   modify standing data
   update
   interrogate
   print

   Such functions should be segregated into different menus. This means that a casual user browsing through the files should not be allowed to insert/delete/modify/update without going into another menu which may be privacy-locked (i.e. a password or code would be required to gain access to that facility).

9. ➤ Passwords are a desirable feature as is the ability to set file production codes and tables on programs and data files*. If the operating system does not allow passwords, they can still be attached to various functions. For example, the insertion of a new employee in a payroll system may require a password or privacy lock. This could be extended to all especially sensitive functions although the ability of an authorised individual to carry around a large number of passwords should not be overestimated.

10. The incorporation of a monitor into the operating system could police it in an absolute way and collect statistics about the activities of the system (e.g. what programs are being run, how many transactions are being input and so on). The same system could pre-empt the use of certain resources in non-legitimate ways.

11. Good accounting logic could be incorporated into the applications software. This is discussed further below.

One problem still not dealt with is the possibility that data files may be taken to another machine where they may become contaminated. However some machine dependent software protection may be incorporated to prevent this, although some of the above features may render this unnecessary (e.g. privacy locks contained in a separate and hidden file).

More advanced software solutions are explained in Appendix 5.

NEW ACCOUNTING SYSTEMS

In addition to the consideration of new hardware and software solutions, some attention must be paid to applications software – in this instance the applications which are of most concern are the set of programs comprising the accounting system. An example of 'good' accounting software is given below.

A good general ledger will retain the information shown in the table at the top of page 56 on a monthly basis and print it out at the end of the accounting period.

There are however more advanced solutions using accounting software which attempt to alter the approach to accounting systems.

---

*By suitable encryption they can be used on floppy discs which have widespread access. However they are irrelevant where one person is the machine operator and there is no segregation of duties (as in a small firm with one bookkeeper).

Account	Current period		Year to date	
	Dr	Cr	Dr	Cr
Code description				
Opening balance			x	
Transaction type plus				
narrative	x			
,,		x		
,,	x			
,,		x		
,,	x			
,,		x		
Period movements	x	x	x	x
Closing balance			x	

The usual computerised approach is to follow the manual system which involves:

source document
↓
entry into prime book
↓
posting to subsidiary and general ledgers

Usually the prime books of entry are the transaction listings which also dovetail with the audit trail.

Using an events accounting system (Sorter, 1969), the original economic event (i.e. transaction plus all relevant evidence pertaining to that transaction) is stored and no further work is carried out. In contrast, in the conventional system, loss of information results as it is aggregated and summarised. In an events system, only the original transactions would be stored in time and date order on a database. (Databases are described in Chapter 5.)

A database management system would then allow the retrieval of these records in different and flexible ways. Obviously it would be desirable to recreate the conventional general ledger accounts of a firm, but it would also be useful to ascertain the effect of a number of transactions on certain balances as well as breaking down a particular account into an opening balance and transactions.

One of the novel forms of re-arranging data is to ask the database to list all the transactions input by a particular person, after 5pm (this would be possible since each entry to a database is often identified uniquely by time).

A simplified form of an events accounting system exists in some packaged software for microcomputers. This software would write all transactions to a file as they are input. Although these transactions may be processed by a client's accounting system, the retention of a transaction file intact forms the basis of a simplified events system.

A true events accounting system has the following characteristics:

1. It concerns itself with storing the maximum amount of information about each event.
2. It does not allow the matching and deletion of paid invoices.
3. It retains all transactions.
4. It uses a sophisticated database facility.

No packaged software provides the types of facilities described by Everest and Weber (1977) or McCarthy (1979).

Approach 6 in Chapter 2 concerned 'the reprocessing of the complete transactions files generated by a client's system' as an acceptable way forward through some of the morass surrounding systems-based auditing. To achieve these advantages a lower order of system equivalent to a transactions file rather than an events file may be all that is necessary.

An events system stores all events (which include transactions) and so it should be easy to match any documents or paperwork to the events in the computer record. In addition, the businessman, who is not educated in accounting, may find the concept of storing events intrinsically easier to grasp and learn.

A second advantage is that by using the enquiry language of a database system, auditors have at their disposal a very powerful extraction and computer audit enquiry facility.

Thirdly, the auditor could always take a copy of the year's events (in the smaller systems, these should fit on one or two floppy discs) and re-perform (i.e. simulate) the processing on the auditor's computer.

For such a system, the reprocessing of a vouched transaction file for the period, by an independent programmer on an independent machine under controlled, independent conditions will provide the auditor with much of the assurance he needs without substantial audit cost or inconvenience to the client. The use of a transactions file rather than a fully developed events accounting system is particularly applicable to computer based accounting systems in small firms. The sole requirement is that the auditor should have a program which is adequate for producing the necessary reports for client data and transaction files, in a known format, readable by the auditor's machine (either from a compatible disc or by means of a network).

Prevention of transaction amendment is still technologically impossible on most floppy disc based systems. Preventing the undetectable correction of errors found in transaction entries is a traditional accounting concern. In the 'events' approach, there are two possibilities:

1. The original event can be amended; or
2. The original event cannot be changed; amendment must be by way of an amendment 'event' and the subsequent creation of a new amended event.

The advantages of vouching to a single correct record in a transaction file need to be weighed against the difficulty and audit cost of vouching perhaps three distinct, and perhaps physically separate, transaction records (e.g. original event, event signalling an error in original event plus a new amendment) against a single externally generated voucher or document. It can be argued that the easy correction of errors may be an advantage that should not be denied to small firms even though this runs contrary to the traditional accounting view.

One possibility arising from the widespread use of events accounting is that the responsibility of management may end with the complete and accurate recording of an event. Someone else, a service bureau (or even a part of the practice undertaking the audit work) may carry out the rest of the data processing work and routine operations.

CONCLUSIONS

Internal controls are important, irrespective of whether auditing is being carried out around or through the computer. Small businesses and their computer systems have notoriously bad internal controls. There are three clearly identified approaches to internal controls outlined in this section.

One avenue of thought suggests the enforcement of minimum standards of control. In an alternative approach we examined ways of retaining the freedom made possible by microcomputers and the benefits that can be derived by using different controls (e.g. the solution whereby management involvement replaces conventional controls). Although such new techniques may compensate for a lack of conventional control, this compensation can never be enough for audit comfort in either auditing around or through a computer system.

The third approach explored represented a more recent and less restrictive methodology using hardware and software solutions, in varying degrees, to improve internal control. Often the computer itself can achieve good results by writing extra information and following procedures in a logical order. However, even with this methodology, some enforcement is necessary; for example, security copying is enforced and certain operations and procedures have to be performed in a specified order and manner.

One particularly promising solution is the events accounting approach which offers the advantage of vouching to a single correct record in a transaction file. Although no events accounting system is commercially available, packaged software offering ledgerless accounting, with reference to conventional files storing all transactions, confers most of the audit advantages of events accounting systems.

It is our opinion that these new hardware and software solutions offer the best way forward. They offer the most secure internal controls within a small business environment and although there is a small 'imposition' on the actions of the personnel running the system (i.e. the owner), this restriction of individual liberty is minimised (the machine performs most of the control) and the advantages of the microcomputer – approachability, flexibility and freedom – are retained. Yet the accountant receives a higher standard of control than ever before in a small business context.

One of the objectives of this report has been to pose the question: can the client, by means of the introduction of the microcomputer, be offered a degree of control where none was possible? The answer is: yes, it can. The hardware and software solutions in the previous section do just that.

5

Small computer applications in the office of the small business and the small practice

INTRODUCTION

Formerly, most small organisations relied on manual accounting methods, some were making use of computer bureaus, others visible record computers and some were using mechanical accounting machines. Now that the cost of small computers has dropped so dramatically, more and more small organisations are installing their own 'in house' computers and therefore fewer are relying on the above methods.

The installation of a small computer within a small organisation will undoubtedly have an impact. This impact is however likely to be different from that made by the introduction of large computers in large organisations in a previous generation. The reasons for this are the different characteristics of both small organisations and small computers.

Small organisations generally have less formal internal structures and a less formal organisation than large concerns. A good deal of the information about the firm is carried in the heads of one or two key personnel. These people are also likely to be aware of most of the activities of the organisation. It follows therefore that key decisions are taken by a small number of people who can communicate more rapidly. Herein lies the advantage of the small organisation, the unrivalled flexibility which stems from a reliance on the human brain and face-to-face communication.

We believe that the growth of a small organisation leads to a breakdown in informal information systems as too many facts exist for one person to grasp and the evaluation of new facts becomes more difficult. As more people become involved in the management of the organisation and as the informal communication system breaks down, important items of information do not necessarily reach those concerned. This results in more frequent crises, a reduction in flexibility and a decline in service to customers or clients. The change from a small to a medium sized organisation with its greater formality represents one of the critical stages of growth. The point of change varies in terms of turnover and of number of employees. However, many small organisations will not pass this point because their success depends on their remaining small. With the development of more formal and rigid systems, they are unable to provide the same service, resulting in the loss of ground to smaller organisations.

Small computers, unlike their older mainframe cousins, are not dominated by the high cost of a central processing unit. In small computers, this unit is generally contained on a single inexpensive chip. In the past, the main feature of a large computer was that an organisation was fitted around the computer in order to make the most efficient use of it. For example, the batch system was developed as an efficient way of using central processor time. The overriding view was that users must provide data when required by the computer and accept it when convenient to the computer. The electronic data processing departments therefore tended to acquire an unjustified status in many organisations.

Such systems may be tolerated in large to medium sized organisations – in other words, where routine and inflexibility occur. In contrast, small computers have two key advantages: their low cost and the ability of the user to gain direct access to the machine, thus bypassing the inflexibility of data processing departments. From these advantages, it follows that the user is under less pressure to make efficient use of the processor and that the variable costs associated with using the computer drop dramatically. The small computer can and does fit into the special organisation and structure of small firms and is expected to be able to cope with an increase in level of activity without affecting the operating characteristics of the firm.

GENERAL COMPUTERISED APPLICATIONS IN THE OFFICE

Currently in the Western economies, users of small computers are focusing their attention on four types of packaged software. These can be classified as follows:

1. Word processing packages.
2. Accounting packages, such as sales ledger, purchase ledger, payroll and so on.
3. Database packages: these vary from simple card index systems to reasonably sophisticated systems.

4. Financial modelling packages, for example either spreadsheet packages or more complex packages known as modelling systems (Grinyer and Wooller, 1975).

1. Word processing packages

Word processors generally come in two forms, either the 'stand-alone' type or a computer with a word processing package. The principle of operation is the same, the difference being that a stand-alone word processor is not capable of performing other tasks that may be undertaken by a small computer. In principle, there is little difference between word processing and data processing. Data processing frequently results in reports being written by a computer containing the necessary information (for example profit and loss accounts). Word processing can be used to produce reports, letters and documents. Given the nature of work in the accountant's office and offices in general, it is easy to see why the word processor has made such a large impact. This view is supported by evidence collected from the case studies.

When using a typewriter, immediate output is produced (typewritten page) in response to a series of key depressions. A word processor, in contrast, stores the input and displays it on a screen retaining an option to produce a typewritten page when instructed by the typist. Whilst the document is displayed on the screen, the typist has the opportunity to insert and delete characters, move portions of text and reformat pages prior to printing out the final document. Different word processors have differing abilities, the most sophisticated incorporating dictionaries which will automatically check spelling.

The minimum characteristics considered necessary for a word processor can be summarised as follows:

(a) Documents should be displayed on a screen whilst being edited.
(b) Pages should be automatically numbered.
(c) Automatic formatting of lists or tables should be possible.
(d) Document page formatting, page length, number and spacing of lines, indentation or paragraphing and margin justification should be available options.
(e) Cursor movements allowing the addition, deletion or alteration of individual lines or words anywhere in the text should be possible.
(f) There should be an ability to move large sections of text around the document.
(g) A 'find and replace' facility should exist; that is, the ability to find a unique combination of characters in the text of a document and replace it with an alternative set of characters.

2. Accounting packages

Generally, accounting packages performing the structured operational tasks in an organisation are the least innovative of all computerised applications. Accounting packages for small computers are now widely available for a variety of environments. It is common for particular software houses to specialise in the problems of a particular trade or profession, producing standardised packages to suit the activities of these types of organisation. There are, for example, several software houses that specialise in providing packages for the accounting profession.

3. Database packages

As a software concept, the database arose in the late 1960's. It mirrored the desire for integrated management systems which were popular at that time. The objective was to maintain all corporate data on one file instead of many, thereby eliminating duplication of information and facilitating the maintenance of that information. The existence of a central pool of information gave rise to the development of software to access the information in any manner specified by the user. At first, databases were confined to mainframe computers due to memory and storage constraints. Now it is possible to purchase database packages to run on most small computers.

Unfortunately, there has been a recent proliferation of so-called database packages which in reality vary from the electronic card index to the true database. These packages can be classified broadly speaking into three categories:

(a) Data management systems.
(b) Hierarchical or network systems.
(c) Relational systems.

The majority of packages available for microcomputers fall into the first category, although there are an increasing number of examples available in the second and third categories.

Data management systems include packages from the very simple electronic card index to the more sophisticated packages that claim to be true databases. Systems at the lower end of this category allow a limited number of reports to be compiled based on the nature of the information recorded. For example such a system could be used to record employee details and could rapidly answer such questions as the following: which employees are earning over £15000, have two children and live in Hampstead?

Systems at the higher end of this category, by contrast, allow much greater manipulation of data and the creation of programs to process it using a form of database query language. These languages, sometimes known as very high level languages (c.f. high level languages such as BASIC), allow many of the features of high level programming languages but are easier to use and can provide much faster solutions to problems than traditional programming methods. Very powerful results can be achieved when used in conjunction with software tools (see below).

4. Financial modelling packages
It is possible to divide financial modelling packages for small computers into three broad categories. These are as follows:

(a)   Electronic spreadsheet programs (usually costing £200 or less).
(b)   Sophisticated spreadsheet programs (usually costing £300-600).
(c)   Full modelling systems (usually costing about £1,000).

(a) Electronic spreadsheet programs
1978 saw the introduction of a new concept in software for small computers, it was a program called Visicalc. Essentially Visicalc comprises a huge matrix of approximately 16,000 cells of which only a small proportion are visible at any one time on the screen (typically 8 columns and 20 rows). The user is able to move a pointer or cursor freely over the entire matrix and, at the particular cell indicated by the pointer, can enter numerical data, alphabetic narrative or mathematical formulae. The mathematical formulae may relate the contents of two different cells to a third cell, and therein lies the power of spreadsheet programs. Their most popular use is in the field of budgeting and financial planning. Many firms set up, in tabular form, projected monthly budgets based on suitable mathematical relationships, in order to ask 'what if' questions. It is possible, for example, to see what would happen to cash balances six months ahead if cash were extracted from debtors more quickly, in say two months time.

Although the theoretical maximum size of most spreadsheets is about 160 cells, in reality only about 1,000 cells (8-bit machines) or 2,000 cells (16-bit machines) may be used for one model. (Any model over this level would require a much more sophisticated package on a mainframe computer.) Initial disadvantages with spreadsheet programs were that each model worked in isolation, so that two models could not be consolidated. Facilities for report writing were very limited, usually being confined to printing out the complete model by displaying figures or formulae. Links with graphics were limited and therefore precluded good illustrations to reports. Finally, even if data was already on file in the computer, the information generally had to be written into the spreadsheet program through the keyboard. To a great extent, many of these disadvantages no longer exist in current spreadsheets although size still remains a constraint on most packages.

These packages were seen by many firms as being so powerful that they purchased small computers merely to run them for modelling purposes. This is only one example of why the purchase decision affecting small computers is, and should be, much more software-oriented than for large computers owing to the relative costs of hardware and software.

(b) Sophisticated spreadsheet programs

The more sophisticated spreadsheets have one chief advantage over the simple spreadsheets. The user is given the opportunity to print reports based on the data held by the program. Therefore a much more flexible result is available by defining the output from the model, and thus being able to create individual report formats. In addition, with linkages to graphics packages, the presentation of data can be much more meaningful to non-financial key personnel in the organisation. New packages tend to combine a comprehensive spreadsheet package with word processing, graphics and database capabilities.

(c) Full modelling systems

Packages in this category can often be in direct competition with the sophisticated spreadsheets but generally cost considerably more. The crucial difference is the greater flexibility which arises, and the ability to cope with more complex logic. For example, the performance of different sets of logic according to the value of certain variables can be undertaken.

Examples of the facilities offered in a modelling system can be found in Bhaskar (1978), Grinyer and Wooller (1975) and Sherwood (1983).

USE OF SOFTWARE TOOLS

Having regard to the type of software being used and also the fact that there is considerable cost pressure on software development, it is apparent that a market for sophisticated software tools has developed in the small computer area. A software tool can be defined as software that speeds up and assists in the process of producing applications software.

Initially these tools took the form of compilers or interpreters which translated human readable instructions (high level languages such as BASIC, and Fortran) into machine readable instructions. Editors, which allowed the preparation of programs in high level languages, quickly followed. Sophisticated text or word processors were the next development. Currently there is a wide range of tools available for small computers, including programs which deal with data entry and sorting, and even databases which allow a limited amount of programming in a very high level language or database query language (see above). The feature of this new breed of software is that a good proportion of the final applications program has been written with its cost being shared out amongst a large number of users. This allows users to aquire virtually custom-made software at a price which is compatible with hardware costs. It is possible for users to take two or more of these 'tools' and to synthesise a workable program that may fulfil their needs at an economic price (see Dearnley, 1982).

USE OF SMALL COMPUTERS IN DISTRIBUTED SYSTEMS

Before the arrival of the cheap small computer, the only way a small firm could have access to computing power was through a time-sharing system. In other words, the firm would pay for time on a computer, usually owned by a large company or a bureau. Such a service had a number of disadvantages; for example, lack of privacy, high variable cost of using the service, lack of control of data and problems of ownership of data in the event of the host company being liquidated.

At this stage it is interesting to consider the possibility of using a small computer to emulate a terminal to a time-sharing system. This would allow the small computer user to have access to the vast facilities and data on a mainframe whilst retaining the ability locally to edit files, maintain storage and process data.

Emulation has however its drawbacks. By using terminal emulation programs files could, for example, be transferred from a mainframe to a small computer. Although many small computers allow this type of operation very few allow other operations concurrently. In addition, the operation is rather cumbersome, involving physical link-ups and the transfer of whole files where only a portion may be required.

The alternative to emulation is to make the files on the mainframe directly accessible to the small computer. In this way, the mainframe system acts as part of the small computer. The result is a system which operates very smoothly with low communication times, since the number of file updates is often small in comparison with file size. To do this, a common operating system is required between computers. Pechura (1981) performed such an experiment using two small computers and a common operating system. He found that this direct access method enhanced the operation of the small computer system. The program execution was always local but with access to almost all data in the network.

At present, many small computers are capable of being connected into networks. Although many small computers are mainframe compatible through emulation programs, those that now support the UNIX operating system for direct links to large computers are not widely available. UNIX has, up to now, not gained ready acceptance by the business community and has been mainly confined to scientific applications. This may change, however.

It is also likely that an alternative operating system with similar features may become accepted for general use in future.

USE OF PUBLIC DATABANKS

Despite their reputation for being costly, public databanks have been available for some time, offering to subscribers a wealth of public information, from stock exchange prices to train timetables. There are many small computers which can be connected to such public databanks. British Telecom has introduced a databank which has electronic mail facilities. In the USA, subscription services are available involving databanks linked in a network giving wide access to information. It is possible to gain access to these public services (for example Dialcom or ARPANET) using a cheaper BBC Micro by going through the Slough switching service and thus by satellite to the USA.

INFORMATION SYSTEMS AND COMPUTERISATION

Despite the apparent proliferation of software, computerisation of activities within firms has made very little real impact on information systems as the following will demonstrate. Using the Gorry and Scott Morton model of an information system, the various activities of an organisation can be classified in the matrix below (see Lucas, 1978).

	Operational	*Management*	*Strategic*
Structured	Time recording Purchase Ledger	Budgets Personnel reports	Office location
Semi- structured	Work in progress records	Analysis of variances	Provision of new client service
Un- structured	Cash management	Management of personnel	Planning for training and research

In this re-interpretation of Lucas' presentation, activities which might be undertaken in accounting practices are used.

As Lucas says, it quickly becomes apparent that only the activities which fall in the top left area of the matrix are generally computerised. In other words the impact of computing on all practices is confined to solving the routine, repetitive and specific tasks. There is increasing evidence, Lucas adds, to support the view that computers can be used to produce greater cost savings in the less structured and more strategic areas of activity.

USE OF COMPUTERS IN THE SMALL PROFESSIONAL ACCOUNTANT'S OFFICE

This chapter has so far given a broad overview of the currently possible and anticipated uses of small computers in small organisations in general. At this point, it is worth examining specifically the environment of the small accounting practitioner and the relevance of these ideas to the development of small practices. The conclusions presented here are partly based on evidence gained from the case studies and partly on experimental research.

A feature of all practices is the division of work into non-chargeable and chargeable categories. The former amounts to practice administration and can be considered as overheads, the latter relates to direct fee-earning work recoverable directly from each client. Examples of practice administration might be: maintenance of clients' records, internal accounting, time-recording, payroll, personnel and recruitment, planning and scheduling, research and technical development, training and office management. Examples of chargeable work would include book-keeping, accountancy, taxation, auditing, investigations, insolvency, company secretarial work, trusts and financial advice.

Whilst these are functions that can exist in all firms, it is worth reiterating that one of the features of smaller firms is that they tend not to have specialised functional departments which perform these activities. For example, small firms will not have personnel or recruitment departments, this function normally being part of the duties of one or all of the partners. Similarly all partners will be expected to carry out, to varying degrees, all types of chargeable work undertaken by the partnership. Generally the nature of work undertaken by small practices is correspondingly different from that of large practices, being oriented much more to the provision of bookkeeping and accountancy services rather than auditing, which appears to represent a greater proportion of the normal work of larger practices.

This distinction naturally arises from the differing requirements of the clients. The work of the small practice amounts in part to the assumption of the roles of part-time accountant and part-time financial director to a small business which is unable to employ full-time personnel to fulfil these functions.

As mentioned in the previous part of this section, whilst there may be potential for computers to be used in solving unstructured strategic problems, at present it is the structured, operational problems for which computers are proving most useful. These activities can be categorised as follows for the small practice:

Non-chargeable	*Chargeable*
Word processing	Word processing
Time recording	Incomplete records and accounts preparation
Payroll	
	Tax computations
Staff scheduling	
	Client accounting services (including the production of management information)
Client records	
Financial, fiscal and legal database	
	Budgeting, cash flow and financial modelling for clients
Budgeting, cash flow and financial modelling	
Partnership accounts	

Word processing

The arrival of word processing has and will continue to have the most fundamental and far reaching practical impact on all practices including the small practice.

In the smaller practising office, the sequence of work for clients generally begins with the preparation of handwritten draft accounts based on the previous year. This is usually typed as a draft set of accounts. After partner-approval, another set of draft accounts may be produced for client-approval. A further and final set of accounts for signature is then produced. Each time a set of accounts is prepared on a typewriter, it is followed by a laborious and costly process often known by trainee accountants as 'calling over'. This is necessary to ensure complete accuracy of typing. Generally, the retyping takes place for only minor typographical alterations, even on a year-to-year basis. The use of a word processor means that vast financial and human cost savings can be made since the bulk of the accounting report only has to be typed and called over once with a number of small alterations at each subsequent stage. Similar cost savings can be made for other reports and documents that may be produced by the firm.

As far as chargeable work is concerned there are several areas where word processors can be used to effect cost savings. Obvious examples are where standard letters are being sent to a variety of addresses during the course of an audit, in accounts preparation such as a debtors' circularisation, or in letters to banks requesting certificates of balances. The preparation of letters of representation or letters of comment is also facilitated by using a word processor.

Time recording

Time recording is one of the most mundane but important tasks in a professional office. It involves the allocation of staff time to either clients or non-chargeable overheads. The purpose of such systems is to provide control of time spent on various jobs and to provide a basis for charging fees through the use of charging-out rates for different categories of staff.

This sort of application is ideally suited to computerisation because it is a process that involves recording data to produce multiple reports by scanning that data in different ways. For example, partners and managers require regular reports on work done on a client basis and also on an employee basis. The preparation of these reports is both time-consuming and costly when done manually, unlike the use of a computer-based system, which simply requires the depression of a few keys.

One potential disadvantage of running time recording packages on small computers is that a large amount of storage is required. For a typical small firm (e.g. Practice 2 in the case studies) of 1,000 clients and 40 staff with 250 working days in the year and 29 quarter-hour time slots per day, a considerable amount of data is generated. However the use of the computer resources is likely to prove much more efficient and economical than equivalent human resources for all sizes of practice.

Payroll

Payroll systems may not be worthwhile on small computers in a small practice for internal purposes alone. One estimate puts the saving in a small practice between a half and one day per week. Payrolls have to be designed to the specifications of the Inspector of Taxes (PAYE) and the Department of Health and Social Security (NI) in addition to the requirements of the firm. Major problems arise annually with changes in legislation and changes in rates of taxation. In addition there are many other variables such as payments made monthly, weekly and hourly and the choice of payment, such as credit transfer, cheque or cash. The situation is however different if the firm chooses to market a payroll service to external users (clients and possibly non-clients). In this case payroll systems may be worthwhile but the degree of maintenance should not be underestimated, although this is reduced by the employment of staff who are comfortable with computers.

Many small firms will find it cheaper and easier to allow a bureau to handle their payrolls given the relative cost of these services compared with the cost of payroll packages, which incur regular annual maintenance costs. Naturally some firms will prefer to retain the preparation of their payroll 'in house' for the benefits of control and privacy. In this case, serious consideration should be given to retaining manual methods.

Staff scheduling

Staff scheduling systems are used by all professional firms as an aid to efficiency. Staff represent one of the most costly resources used by firms and their efficient use is important in achieving not only cost savings, but client satisfaction (matching suitable staff to each job) and maintaining staff morale.

These systems vary from the very formal in large firms to the extremely informal in small firms. They are concerned with optimising the use of staff by experience and qualifications, ensuring the correct priority of jobs and minimising other factors such as travelling time to clients' premises and idle time. The potential benefits of computerising such systems in larger firms are obvious, and have already been widely realised. The case for smaller firms is not so strong, given that partners have a closer and more informal contact with staff and that the characteristics and strength of the small firm are based on its flexibility and ability to make rapid decisions due to face-to-face communications and the lack of formal systems. Partners and administrators in small firms have an easier and more comprehensive overview of the resources of their firm.

Client records

The potential for computerising client records (e.g. audit files and tax files) appears at present to be largely undeveloped. It is envisaged that in the near future, rather than maintaining information in the traditional, handwritten audit or tax files, audit clerks will visit premises with portable microcomputers. These machines would not only perform the role of audit files but would also be available to take an active part in the audit itself (e.g. interrogation of the client's computer). Such a view is technically feasible now but, as with the concept of the 'paperless office', it may prove difficult to implement due to economic or sociological barriers.

However, many practices both large and small already maintain part of their client records (typically accounts from the previous year) on a computer or at a minimum on an automatic typewriter. The advantages of doing this are apparent when considered as part of a word processing system for the production of final accounts. Whilst some of the larger firms may be considering moving towards the maintenance of audit files on computer, it is unlikely that this would be appropriate for small firms in view of the high cost of maintaining an 'in house' computer sufficiently large for their requirements. If small firms were to use a bureau or timesharing system for this purpose, problems of confidentiality of data in the event of a crisis in the bureau are likely to arise.

Financial, fiscal and legal databases
As mentioned earlier in this section, public databanks are becoming available which can provide a range of information that might be useful for accountants in practice. Small practices are likely to need information in the following areas:

(a) Share and loan-stock prices, details of dealings and historical information on listed companies and gilt edge stock.
(b) Details of case law surrounding income tax, corporation tax and value added tax.

There are a number of possible organisations which could provide such a service. The first and most obvious is the ICAEW itself acting as a central fund of fiscal and financial data. However, the provision of such a service would require a relatively large investment for the Institute both in terms of computing power and manpower to ensure that information is properly maintained. The Institute may feel that it is not prepared to take such a risk on behalf of smaller practices. However, this would be a beneficial and useful role which the Institute could play in helping and fostering the small practice.

Another possible solution is that large firms maintaining such data might be prepared to sell information to small firms in order to recover some of their costs. Finally, some independent commercial body could provide such information either through their own database or via a public databank service.

Budgeting, cash flow and financial modelling

All organisations, including accounting practices, can operate more efficiently with information concerning future projected cash flows, budgets and financial models. In the smallest organisations, planning in these terms takes place informally and is often unrecorded. Naturally, this ad hoc approach to planning can produce problems. For example, the possible long term effects of short term decisions are not anticipated.

There are a variety of modelling packages available for micro-computer systems as previously mentioned. Therefore even the smallest practice can derive substantial benefits from packages at the lower end of the range. Simple spreadsheet programs at less than £200 probably produce the best returns in terms of costs and benefits for the small practice, not only for internal cash flow forecasting and budgeting but also for providing a similar service for clients. In addition these packages are so flexible that they can be used for non-financial purposes such as simple job cost estimating in manufacturing or engineering applications on behalf of, or by, clients. The more sophisticated packages in the range £500 to £1,000 tend to be less flexible and more dedicated to financial modelling and whilst showing relatively lower cost benefit returns are more appropriate to the small to medium size firm.

However it should be remembered that it still requires some degree of expertise to build a useful financial model using a modelling package.

Partnership accounts

Accounting packages, though varying in quality and price, are available for partnership accounting purposes. Initially, the quality of many accounting packages was very poor but with increasing competition and customer awareness, better quality systems have emerged. It is worth pointing out that computerised facilities for internal accounts purposes will often be beneficial, but for the very small practice, or even the very small business, the acquisition of computerised facilities purely for internal accounts purposes may not always be particularly beneficial. On the other hand, if a computer is acquired for additional reasons, for example, as an aid to decision-making or revenue generation, then computerising the internal accounts is usually beneficial.

Incomplete records and accounts preparation

The preparation of accounts forms a large percentage of the work undertaken by small practices. Accounts preparation can be undertaken from a wide variety of starting points. At one extreme is the 'brown paper parcel' category whilst at the other end is the complete and properly documented trial balance extracted from a set of double entry accounts.

The 'brown paper parcel' is a euphemism used by accountants to describe the situation where a client presents them with bank statement, cheque stubs and a few invoices, previously in a paper bag, now usually a plastic carrier bag! At a minimum, however, accountants will try to encourage their clients to maintain a proper record of cash receipts and payments with supporting vouchers and if the client is large enough to be registered for VAT, Customs and Excise will insist that adequate records are maintained to support VAT returns.

Many firms use small computers to help prepare accounts from incomplete records and in fact this probably rivals word processing in being the first computerised application to be established in accountants' offices. The comparison is interesting in that word processing facilities are often added to the final stage of an incomplete records package to facilitate final accounts preparation as mentioned previously.

Incomplete records packages generally rely on a considerable amount of manual preparation before data is entered into the system. This usually takes the form of a summarisation based on an analysis or classification of the client's transactions. At this stage, the computer can be used to process the data and produce final accounts in one operation. Completely computerised systems starting with raw accounting data are virtually unknown since a manual summarisation process can generally be performed more efficiently by the small practice. However, one firm of those in the case study (see practice 5 in Chapter 6) has been actively trying to develop such a system which requires its clients to maintain their raw accounting data on a microcomputer system which is either compatible with or identical to the practice's computer. When accounts are required this data can be transferred (probably on a floppy disc) to the practice for admission to an incomplete records system. Such a concept can also prove useful for client accounting purposes, for example, the preparation of VAT returns.

Taxation
The majority of calculations surrounding tax computations (income tax, corporation tax, capital transfer tax and capital gains tax) have evolved into a number of standard formats which tend to change marginally each year with successive Finance Acts. Although this report has not specifically addressed itself to taxation questions, it is apparent that there is considerable scope for using small computers to assist in the calculation of taxation liabilities. (At the 1983 ICAEW Summer Conference, Philip Hardman and Alan Bliss illustrated the possibilities of tax law databases and computational software packages.) In addition, there must be the possibility of using taxation models in a similar fashion to financial

models in order to assist in tax planning. We feel (from experimental work conducted at UEA) that even the simplest types of modelling systems, such as spreadsheets, could be configured for these purposes.

Client accounting
In addition to incomplete records and accounts preparation, the provision of accounting services forms a major part of small practice work. Given the nature and administrative limitations of small businesses, there is considerable scope for accountants to provide and expand computerised accountancy work in the manner of a bureau on behalf of their clients. There is no reason to suppose that such a service should be limited purely to recording and accounts preparation. Further possibilities exist in the information and decision making areas. For example, accounting practices could provide management accounts, budgets, and planning and forecasting services. With unincorporated businesses, there should be no barrier to expanding in this area except for the possible competition from other organisations such as a major clearing bank which has recently entered this field. With small incorporated businesses, unresolved ethical problems may arise when the accountant is also performing the audit. If the audit requirement for small companies was removed, this would clarify the situation and allow the possibility of greater overall expansion.

We now consider a number of case studies where practices have (or have not, in one case) introduced various types of computer applications.

6

Case studies

INTRODUCTION

During the course of the project, a number of small firms of practising accountants were visited. The experiences of six different practices are documented in this section and it is hoped that this will prove useful to firms considering computerisation and provide comfort to those that have already embarked on that course. The case studies reported below are representative of a wider cross-section of firms visited.

For reasons of confidentiality the names of each of the firms have been concealed, they are identified consistently throughout the report as Practice 1, Practice 2, . . . Practice 6. Appendix 6 contains detailed descriptions and profiles of each of the six practices. The practices vary from the medium sized practice down to the sole practitioner; three are based in London and three are provincial firms.

Practices 1 and 4 were London based partners and although they were large in absolute terms, they were considered relatively small in London terms. Practices 2 and 3 were provincially based partnerships and had a number of branches. Each branch had a smaller sub-set of partners supervising the branch and the 'branch' was in essence a small practice with only about 2-10 employees. Practices 5 and 6 were one-partner practices.

One of the possible criticisms of the cross-section of practices reported here is that we have not covered the truly small professional firm with, say, under 24 employees. Although the first four practices have greater than 24 employees the structure and client profile of practices 2 and 3 make them amenable to classification as small.

Another potential criticism is that many of the practices have chosen machines which involve hard rather than floppy disc systems. This is in essence what was found across a much larger cross-section: no example of a firm using multiple microcomputers with floppy systems were found. As to whether their choice of machine was correct or not, we simply reported on what was found. It must be remembered that the current generation of microcomputers were not being marketed in a timescale that made it possible for us to report on real production usage during the period under study (i.e. 1981-2).

EXPERIENCES OF COMPUTER APPLICATORS

Practice 1 (14 partners)

This practice faced a crucial decision during 1980. Its five year old cassette-based visible record computer had become unreliable and was incurring high maintenance costs. In addition, it would shortly require a major refurbishment at further cost and the supplying company had indicated that no further development work would be carried out on this particular model. The maximum life expectancy of the computer was two years.

The practice was unhappy with the performance of the computer for the following reasons:

(a) There was inadequate capacity on the system which was aggravated by the slow speed of a cassette-based system.
(b) There were difficulties in using a remote system, this was experienced by all offices apart from the main office where the computer was located.
(c) The slow processing of small final adjustments to accounts and the poor quality of the printer meant that it could not be used for final accounts.
(d) No adequate bookkeeping programs existed.

After some consideration, the practice decided to purchase a new computer system and drew up a list of desirable attributes that such a system might have. These included the following:

(a) Client accounting: The system should include an incomplete records system and a facility for the preparation of statutory accounts with the opportunity of direct access from remote offices. It must be capable of processing several tasks simultaneously and at least 80 per cent of accounts should be computerised. It was essential to be able to produce final accounts from trial balances using word processing facilities and avoiding the use of secretaries.
(b) Time recording: Regular reports were required every two or three weeks showing activity reports by partner, group and employee. Such a system was also to include client disbursements.
(c) Fees ledger package: The practice wanted this on-line with the facility to update it daily.

(d) Payroll package: The firm already operated a payroll system as a bureau service to clients and naturally wanted this to continue on the new computer.

(e) Word processing: Facilities were required for the production of standard documentation and letters such as bank letters, engagement letters, etc.

(f) Bookkeeping: The firm wanted a system which would provide clients with either monthly or quarterly management accounts.

(g) Internal accounts: With suitable privacy protection on output, the firm wanted to be able to maintain internal accounts on the computer.

(h) Solicitor's accounting package: The firm already provided a bureau service for solicitors and wished to continue this service on the new computer, possibly providing an on-line (terminal and printer) service to at least one main client.

(i) Communication facilities: A cost-effective means of transferring information between offices was felt to be desirable. This could be achieved with on-line terminals to the computer in the main office.

Two approaches to the problem were adopted. The first involved the use of a central computer based at the main office with terminal links via British Telecom leased lines to the other offices. Typically one or more VDUs and a printer would be located at the remote offices. The chief disadvantage of this system was the vulnerability of the central computer to breakdown and consequent paralysis of the entire system. The alternative approach was the use of individual computers located at each office without communications facilities. Whilst such a system was less vulnerable to breakdown, more operators would be required and it would be less flexible.

After consideration, the first approach was favoured and five companies were approached for quotations.

Eventually the practice awarded the contract to a company which indicated that about six months would be needed for the installation of hardware and software before the process of implementation and conversion from manual procedures could begin. Within two to three years from the date of installation, it was expected that 80 per cent of unincorporated clients would have their accounts produced on the computer. The practice would lose about four typists during this time through natural wastage. The payroll service was expected to run immediately after installation.

The cost of acquiring and running the computer was to be controlled by treating it as a separate office and arranging internal charges to client accounts and users of the service. The capital costs were financed by lease. Total annual running costs, which included lease payments, were about two thirds of the initial capital costs.

The system which is now installed has a greater capacity than initially envisaged. The practice had originally decided on a machine with 128K memory: this was upgraded by a further 256K of memory and the practice was hoping to upgrade it eventually to 1MB. The hard discs originally specified totalled 96MB, being five fixed and one removable. The firm had acquired an additional fixed hard disc of 160MB. Seven VDUs and four printers were used at various locations in the practice.

The firm was very pleased with its system which worked exceedingly well. In particular, with reference to the question of vulnerability to breakdown, they were pleased with the workings of the telephone diagnostics service used by the supplier. There was some concern however in the practice that the conversion process took longer than expected because of the flexibility of the system. The case studies as a whole indicated that the less flexible a system, the more quickly it tends to show cost savings due to a reduced set-up cost and training period. Achieving the right balance is a problem, given that the life of a computerised system is typically five years, but possibly less.

Practice 2 (9 partners)

This practice was an unwilling entrant to the field of computers and it was only the energy and encouragement of one of the partners which finally convinced the partnership of the benefits of computerisation.

Following a rather cautious approach, the firm purchased a system for one of its subsidiary offices in 1980. The firm received good support from the supplier and, despite the fact that both the computer and the printer had to be replaced shortly after installation, the system has proved reliable. The firm later purchased a second system for another subsidiary office. The systems cost in the region of £13,000 and it was estimated that up to £7,000 worth of chargeable time was lost through training. The partnership expected to recover all costs over five years.

Initially after installation, the firm used the computer for incomplete records and accounts preparation which represented a large proportion of work undertaken at the branch offices. Transaction data was acquired from the clients in various forms, summarised and analysed to a standard format for input to the computer. The end result was a set of final accounts achieved by processing through an accounts package with a combined word processing package. Additionally, the firm had been experimenting with a pilot time recording system. After a number of months, it was possible to analyse computer usage approximately as follows:

Idle time	Between 1/2 to 2/3 of the working day
Chargeable time	Up to 1/3 of the working day
Non-chargeable time used	Up to 1/6 of the working day
Maintenance and back-up	Up to 1/6 of the working day

Despite the seemingly high proportion of idle time the computer was showing immediate cost savings which in most cases allowed the initial set-up cost of conversion from the manual system to the computerised system to be absorbed in the first year. The relative inflexibility of the system compared with the system used by Practice 1, no doubt, also contributed to this by reducing set-up procedures. Another point that arose was the relatively high proportion of computer time taken up with time-recording (virtually all the non-chargeable time above).

The firm was in the midst of its second cycle or second year of use when we interviewed it and it expected substantial cost savings to arise in the absence of set-up costs. Furthermore, it was now considering the installation of a computerised system in its main office.

The main office was already wired to facilitate the movement of terminals from office to office once a system had been chosen.

Prior to its introduction, the main motivation for computerisation was to reduce the costs associated with employing low grade staff in the practice. Many small practices rely on relatively large numbers of unqualified staff performing routine tasks. The chief benefit of installing a computer was felt to be the replacement of constantly rising future salaries and wages with the more fixed and predetermined running costs of a computer. In effect, the practice was buying forward in the labour market.

Practice 3 (15 partners)
This practice first bought a computer in 1979. For some time they had been using a time recording system at a bureau but had become increasingly dissatisfied with the package. A specification for a new time-recording system was developed and the practice asked a number of bureaus to quote for the bespoke development of the package. All the bureaus approached proved to be too expensive. Several computer manufacturers were then approached.

Originally, all available systems were too inflexible for this practice but the supplier was willing to modify and develop the product.

The system developed in 1979 satisfied 60 per cent of the practice's requirements but it took a further 3 years to cover the last 40 per cent satisfactorily. The practice are reasonably satisfied with the final product.

The initial hardware was based on a computer with 2×4.8 megabyte cartridge discs. In December 1980, the system was upgraded to incorporate a computer with 256KB memory and 2×40 megabyte discs. A fixed hard disc has also been added with a capacity of 134 megabytes. The system currently has 12 VDUs and 5 printers.

The first applications software to be mounted was the payroll followed by the fees ledger and time recording and later the various ledgers. The system was enhanced in 1980 to take care of the practice's word processing requirements and to provide additional capacity for incomplete records and clients' services work.

The set of applications currently operated on the computer is:

All the practice's ledgers.
Time recording and fees ledger.
Payroll.
Word processing.
Accounts typing.
Incomplete records.

A novel feature is client services – a data processing bureau-type service to clients. This raises some £50,000 of annual fee income and is growing rapidly. The client services include payroll, ledger, word processing of mailing lists, clients who issue rent demands, and management accounting applications.

On the client services payroll system, the practice has 50 clients who go directly to a payroll clerk who uses a VDU to input data. The service is complete including the production of P45s, P60s and P11Ds.

Much attention has been paid to offering clients a complete data processing service with carefully designed forms, good control procedures, and a variety of reports providing good management information.

An incomplete records system requires much careful thought if services are to be provided to a client in a cost effective way. There are some 150 incomplete records clients in the computer system of this practice. In general, the practice follows three steps in incomplete records jobs:

1. Planning of the approach.
2. Analysis of information and deciding what can be input to the computer.
3. Review.

The computer cannot help with steps 1 and 3. In step 2, the decision is sometimes made to input a summary based on a certain amount of manual analysis. With some clients, all the bank transactions are input individually and the computer analyses the coded bank statements.

The final accounts are not produced directly from the incomplete records system as the simultaneous use of the word processing system is beyond the capacity of the machine. So the incomplete records system produces a draft set of accounts in poor format. (No trial balance is produced because the system ensures automatic balancing.) This draft set of accounts then forms the basis for the normal accounts preparation on the word processor.

Accounts preparation is a major task for both incomplete and complete records work. The computer produces a skeleton with the correct dates and comparatives brought forward. Blanks are left for the current year's figures which are subsequently added manually. These figures are then keyed in and a neat report is produced on B3 paper using a high quality printer which is then reduced to A4.

Step 2 above might be broken down into two types of operations:

(a) Manual analysis which calls for a degree of professional judgement.
(b) Keying information into the system, an operation which requires a lower level of staff skill.

Because of this, the various types of work have been allocated among different departments in physically separate locations. The accounts preparation and word processing systems are in one department, the client services form a second centre and the incomplete records/practice administration constitutes a third. The level of technical ability in the accounts preparation and word processing department is low, whilst that in the other two departments is higher.

Practice 4 (9 partners)
In 1970 the firm decided to mechanise through a bureau. This subsequently proved to be unsatisfactory: it was inefficient and there were unsatisfactory controls in the package. The practice then developed one package (instead of a series of packages) to deal with the accounts of sole traders and limited companies. One of the partners designed, wrote and implemented the package. This package took about 4 months of development time representing approximately 100 actual hours. It was used for a couple of years but the firm was unhappy with the standard layout of accounts and because the bureau charge was expensive, the practice did not store as much information as was necessary for the application to be completely successful.

In late 1978, the practice bought its first computer – a small micro-based machine. This was purchased to perform client accounting (i.e. the production of client accounts). The prime documents (such as cash book) were entered either by transactions with codes or by analysed summaries. This system is still used currently on two stand-alone computers. The work is classified into three types:

Very incomplete records.
Partially incomplete records.
Complete records.

In using the firm's packages, flexibility was an important consideration. The whole of a file would be given to an operator, with an understanding of bookkeeping, who could enter the information without using standard input forms incorporating pre-prepared data. This practice, unlike others, had only one department dealing with all input and processing of client accounts. The technical staff were well disciplined into working within the three classifications (very incomplete, partially incomplete and complete records) and provided the information and notes in such a way that it could be understood by non–technical computer operators. The manager of this department had considerable bookkeeping skills and was a professionally qualified (certified) accountant who could deal with any remaining problems.

Very incomplete records were defined as having the following records available: bank statements, cheque book stubs, petty cash book and vouchers. Some headings on the bank statements had sufficient items to be pre-listed and input in total.

Partially incomplete records usually had available an analysed cash book, an analysed bank statement, cheque book stubs and vouchers. Most information was input in summary form.

The definition of complete records required a full set of books which should include: cash book, petty cash book, sales day book, purchase day book, wages books, journal entries, prepayments and debtors totals, accruals and creditors totals.

There was a management accounting section that was wholly involved in preparing data processing-type work for clients and providing contract payroll services. The emphasis in this department was on getting the client to do as much work as possible.

As well as contract payroll, the firm has experimented with sales and purchase ledger work for clients. To operate as a bureau service, the firm had to decide what the practice would and would not do. One of the most difficult problems proved to be codes and coding (for example product codes, customer codes). The sales and purchase ledger work turned out not to be cost effective although the practice has not had similar problems with their contract payroll. One of the reasons why the sales and purchase ledger application was unsuccessful could have been the limited capacity of the computers and the inflexibility of the software package.

The final application to be mounted on the computer was the office costing and time recording system for over 2,000 clients. However there was insufficient disc storage for all the firm's clients.

A decision to buy a new machine was taken in 1981 and the machine was delivered in the same year. One of the reasons for purchasing the new computer was to have one machine which would do all the general processing and word processing work. The alternative was a proliferation of machines and computers throughout the office.

The word processing function was used extensively. For example, all tax clients receive a slightly tailored letter at the same time. About 1,600 tailored letters could be processed and envelopes printed in less than a day. The practice commented that whilst the new word processing system was more than adequate there were a few glaring omissions (e.g. centering facilities, decimal tab, no column move or swapping facility). The suppliers have told the practice that they will look into these problems.

After word processing, the practice implemented payroll (including contract payroll) and then transferred their office costing and time recording system to the new system. The new office costing system produces a variety of reports from summary to detailed information. Management can also get more information when billing a client.

The next step the practice took was to transfer some of their client accounting to the new computer from the old one (the systems are similar). Hardware problems with the new computer coupled with difficulties stemming from financial problems of the suppliers slowed the transfer of work. The old machines had a stable, well-developed and bug-free software and with two machines, some work could always be processed, irrespective of hardware problems. If all the firm's work was transferred to the new machine and it broke down, then the firm's work would come to a standstill.

The firm decided to transfer some of their larger clients whose circumstances were changing very drastically. But the set-up time was quite lengthy. For smaller clients, it was cheaper to produce profit and loss and the balance sheet on the old machine. The new computer could be used to produce the full set of statutory accounts (as the word processing functions were more powerful); the old and new machines are therefore used jointly for some clients.

Existing clients are charged for the setting-up time spent on the new computer. Sometimes it is spread over several years on the assumption that in following years it will be possible to do the job more efficiently. The firm estimates that there is a 30 per cent reduction in the time taken to produce accounts and that the set-up cost is always recovered in the second year.

This saving is reduced by the computer costs and an increase in the time of senior staff reviewing work. There is consequently only about a 15 per cent net reduction in costs for this practice. For the client there will probably be an even smaller drop in fees, but there are other intangible benefits. There is an increase in the account detail, greater reliability of the service and more standardised working papers. Since the firm is using less labour there is some expectation that in the future the firm's fees may be maintained (or even fall) in real terms.

Other applications include a client indexing system. The practice has developed this system with an index of clients' names and addresses and associated information for the purpose of (a) printing lists of clients (under different classifications) for reference purposes; (b) printing labels addressed to clients; and (c) personally addressing and printing standard letters to clients. This software is marketed by an associated company which is, in essence, a software house.

The acquisition of the new machine has made it possible to offer a much better computer bureau service. Client services include: tax applications; foreign exchange schedules; full sets of company accounts; departmental management accounts; and management reports with budgets, variances and ratios.

The management accounting service is a major growth area. Either completed input sheets are filled in from various books of account (cash book, petty cash book, purchase ledger, sales ledger, but no nominal ledger) or day books are analysed. For the practice, the big advantage gained by producing monthly management accounts is that they are also doing preparatory work for the year end accounts. When producing the management accounts, the practice can also perform a critical review on an exception basis for a client.

The firm has utilised two other computer applications. One is a quick exercise on whether a husband and wife should elect for separate assessment of the wife's earned income for tax purposes. The other involves reporting investment income for tax returns. All sources of income are listed in a word processor and stored; and in the following year, a copy of last year's dividend list is produced omitting dates and amounts and providing a skeleton. With the client's current dividend vouchers (in alphabetical order) the new information can be written onto the skeleton. Any changes in the investments can be investigated and the skeleton altered manually. The skeleton's new information can be input to the computer which can then do the arithmetic and repetitive printing.

Practice 5 (1 partner)

This small firm, originally comprising 2 partners, became firmly committed to microcomputers at an early stage. In 1978, the firm began collaborating with a local software house to develop a time-recording system for small professional practices. The system has now been successfully developed and marketed. More recently, the firm has been trying to produce an incomplete records package in collaboration with a software house, but finds that inadequate capitalisation of the development is hindering progress. Software development costs are enormous and have a high level of risk attached to them. Whether it is feasible for small firms to develop and market software is questionable. This firm has however been successful with its time-recording system.

The incomplete records package is ambitious in concept. It is anticipated that clients will maintain a computer to record their basic raw data. Periodically, either the data will be transferred on a floppy disc to the accountant's office or, perhaps preferably, the accountant will take his own program on a floppy disc to the client's premises and the required accounting reports can be produced. This is very much akin to Approach 6 in Chapter 2.

Surprisingly, within this firm only one application, time-recording, has been computerised. The firm is very keen to implement both an incomplete records system and a word processing system, but so far has not done this.

Practice 6 (1 partner)

Practice 6 is a small practice that has neither the necessary specialisation of functions nor the inclination to computerise. Following discussions with the partner it is fairly evident that he has shied away from work involving computers.

The types of work which could be performed by such a practice include:

1.   Tax returns and Schedule D work. A computer could undertake:
     (a) A word processing function.
     (b) A calculator function.
     (c) An information function (e.g. information on depreciating assets could be kept).
2.   Some sole traders and small businesses use the practice to perform a secretarial function. Much of this work could be analysed on a computer but the cost of inputting the information would rule this out. Only if the client could fill in the 'inputs' and 'outputs' to his business

in machine readable form would this be economical.
3. There is a small possibility that a practice such as this could run and offer a payroll service to its clients.

CONCLUDING REMARKS

The experiences of the firms dealt with in the case studies varied between a simple and straightforward introduction to computerisation, and a protracted and lengthy introduction. Whatever their experiences in the short term, all the firms which used computers were eventually reasonably satisfied with their systems.

Many of the problems appear to be caused by inadequate planning – lack of a clear idea at the outset of exactly what is to be computerised and the effect of computerisation. This problem is not confined to accounting practices. Indeed many small businesses, through inexperience, overlook the areas that would benefit from computerisation and focus on inappropriate areas. This is mainly at the encouragement of computer salesmen who do not have an understanding or sympathy with the particular trade, profession or small organisation concerned. For example, computerised applications are generally most cost effective when different reports are produced by scanning and/or performing calculations on the same data. For this reason, computers are very effective when used as part of an information or decision making process, in which case the likely results of several proposed courses of action can be assessed.

Routine processing of information for the ultimate production of one report is not so effective, especially for small organisations. A good example of this is the preparation of accounts from incomplete records where a word processing package is not included. The use of a computer for incomplete records production facilitates easier entry of adjustments and may be justified without the addition of a word processing package. Likewise, a package which provides only a word processing facility can be viable in terms of cost. However, the combination of both functions on a computer produces economies of scale and is more cost effective than either function alone.

Firms considering computerisation usually have their interest aroused by perceiving the cost savings to be gained from word processing. They progress from this point to other applications with the objective of reducing low grade and non-qualified personnel. Unfortunately, if this progress is unplanned, the firm can quickly find that it reaches the limits of the capacity of its equipment especially if it subsequently introduces a computerised time recording system. Expansion has its own problems, software is not always portable between different machines and re-implementation of an existing computerised system on new hardware can be both very expensive and disruptive.

Another problem that became apparent was obtaining the right balance of flexibility in applications software. Inflexible software can fail to meet the requirements of the firm causing it to adapt its own procedures to that of the computer system. Highly flexible software on the other hand can require extensive tailoring to the needs of a firm which can be time consuming and expensive.

The case studies suggest that some professional offices have already installed computer systems to automate manual accountancy work that had previously been performed for clients. From this arises a natural extension into offering a wide selection of computer bureau services. A firm newly establishing a bureau must be aware that the bureau would attract work away from that already handled in other ways by the practice as well as perhaps attracting work from other practices or satisfying a previously unfilled demand. At the same time we found an increase in usage of microcomputers in general by the clients of all the practices. This poses some contradictions in terms of strategy for the professional practice in that the client base is gearing itself up with microcomputers whilst at the same time some practices are forecasting that there is a vast potential market for professional based computer bureaus. This apparent contradiction is discussed in the next chapter.

It is important to consider whether the information technology 'revolution', which is supposed to be an aid to business, is actually capable of benefitting the accounting profession.

In the next chapter, we shall look at this question more closely and consider the various aspects of the issues which have already been touched upon.

7

Opportunities to assist clients and improve productivity

INTRODUCTION

In this section we attempt to bring together some of the strands developed earlier in Chapters 2 to 6, in order to provide an integrated list of the new opportunities, created by the advent of microcomputers and their use by both clients and small practices.

The first way in which clients may be helped is through the pegging or lowering of fees for the provision of standard services. The features described below are aimed at reducing costs and/or increasing productivity with this aim in mind. The level and quality of service may also improve. The accounting firm which, through the use of technology, can offer a better service at a lower cost will have a distinctive edge over its less innovative competitor.

COST REDUCTION AND PRODUCTIVITY

In Chapter 5, a number of non-chargeable uses of microcomputers were advocated. These included all the features of the electronic office for example:

Word processing.
Data processing.
Ad hoc (informal) retrieval.
Numerical computations.

In trying to provide a framework of possibilities for the practitioner, the following areas should be considered:

1. General electronic facilities for offices. These include electronic telephone switching, electronic telexing with automatic recall of

memory, microfiching of records, electronic mail and messages, diaries and so on.

2. Word processing of letters. Individual letters tailored by either manual input or through parameters on the client's file (or a combination of both) which can be sent to all clients or categories of clients. Examples of such a process include letters to all tax clients concerning their annual return and the information that they should bring (or send) to the firm.

3. A second type of word processing (plus memory) involves such items as accounts preparation where a skeleton is produced annually with the comparatives being moved across. (This may be called document preparation.) A similar type of function could be provided for schedules to tax returns and possibly for the tax return itself (although Inland Revenue permissson would be needed to draw up a more appropiate form for use by word processing printers). The great advantage of producing a skeleton tax return is that all the deductions (e.g. professional subscriptions) could be prompted on input.

Similar functions can be performed for all records, (very incomplete, incomplete, and full records systems). Schedule D work and dividend listings would benefit similarly.

4. Continuing with tax returns, there are other cost-saving devices:

(a) Building society and bank interest received could be accessed direct from the building society or bank computer via data communications through the telephone network (although this is somewhat hypothetical at present) – this poses problems of confidentiality.

(b) A similar operation could be performed for dividends using a hypothetical central dividend record scheme – this also poses problems of confidentiality.

(c) Calculations for tax and other decisions (e.g. splitting of husband's and wife's tax assessment) could be performed.

(d) A data bank and information retrieval function on tax law (including cases) and recently accepted practice by various tax offices could also be recorded, either via a Prestel-type service or some other central databank. The information could be downloaded to a floppy disc which would be regularly updated.

5. The recording of the accounting firm's own records is an obvious possible source of productivity improvements. As with any good management information system, this would ensure partners were well informed about all aspects of their business and should lead to

better decisions. Variance analysis and good management accounts could prove invaluable.

6. The microprocessor could also be used in a decision support role to help the accounting firm (a) extract information for decisions, and (b) develop financial models and business plans.

7. Manpower planning systems and work scheduling (i.e. the scheduling of available staff time over existing jobs and the scheduling of jobs according to priority and size) should help to improve capacity utilisation, productivity of the staff and client relations.

8. However (7) above is not sufficient. A firm needs to know the profitability of individual staff (and categories of staff) as well as the profitability of individual types of work (e.g. audit, tax, consultancy, secretarial, data processing, special, and so on). In this way, given the existing manpower, the accounting firm can minimise its costs and maximise its profits.

    (*Note:* the potential for (7) and (8) in the very small practice is slight.)

9. The last item is an extension of some of the items developed previously. The creation of databanks on clients, tax and financial information, coupled with an interrogation facility will allow further cost reduction and productivity gains. Included under this heading is information storage of all client details and tax returns with such items as tax rates, and possibly some non-quantitative information such as tax codes (*note:* overlap with 4).

Care must be taken to ensure that such facilities produce cost savings. In one of the practices studied, word processing facilities to save secretarial time would not have been cost effective, since the secretarial service was not fully utilised. A secretary was, however, necessary to perform the roles of telephonist and receptionist, despite the fact that these roles took up only a fraction of her time.

For the small practice to receive the benefits of the above productivity aids, some form of bureau-type service or some certified standard product may be needed.

Another way in which some of the benefits of these services may be gained by smaller practices is that several one or two-partner firms might combine to share a common telephonist/receptionist, word processing and computerised practice administration facilities. However, the distinction between this type of organisation and a larger but loosely-knit partnership is not clear.

Cost-cutting and productivity are only two ways of gaining a competitive edge. Another is to offer an expanded range of chargeable services. Possible opportunities in this area are considered next.

NEW FEE INCOME OPPORTUNITIES

It has been noted that there is no natural boundary for accounting: accounting is what the users of accounting demand. We believe the users are asking for a range of new services and functions which are only partially being met by the Profession.

Some examples of these new services and functions are now considered:

Assistance in the purchase and installation of small business systems

We have found, at one extreme, examples of farmers seeking advice on the purchase of a computer basically to perform the function of a calculating machine. On the other extreme a small business (turnover of £1 million plus), had obtained 'board' approval to spend £5,000 to install a multiple terminal computer to perform: order entry, stock control, all financial and management accounting functions, word processing, computer graphics and so on. (Given the volume of transactions and the nature of the business, such an ambitious project would have required a large mainframe and many man-years of bespoke software effort.)

There is a distinct gap between people's perception of what a computer can do and the actual price/performance combination available to them. With the impact of advertising, some of it grossly misleading, the small businessman is in urgent need of advice.

Who better to turn to than his accountant? Consequently, a new service which could be provided by accountants might be assistance in the purchase and installation of a small business system. Some of the features of such a service have already been mentioned but they include: the analysis of what the individual business actually needs and what is cost-effective – a classic systems analysis job (though simplified in order to minimise costs).

From this follows the next phase, which is advice and help in selecting and implementing the appropriate equipment and technology. This includes supervision and monitoring of any bespoke software (including perhaps the initial specification) as well as acceptance testing of the total system.

Pre-audit considerations of security, integrity and internal control will be paramount. However even within an existing system, advice on internal control, security and efficiency of processing may become a new source of fee income.

Similarly, with existing systems, a new service may be a consultancy to evaluate the quality and quantity of management information emerging from the system and the accounting firm may be responsible for producing suitable documentation. In the event of sudden personnel changes, the accounting firm may have the knowledge to run a back-up service, i.e. the practice's personnel could process the normal transactions of the business on the client's computer (for a fee) until replacement personnel were found and sufficiently trained.

The above can be summarised as a systems analysis role; advice on the economics of computers, installation and implementation of a client's computer system and advice on the controls to be incorporated into a client's computer system.

Data processing bureau work

Much has already been said about this type of work with extensive coverage in the case studies. Initially a firm may 'drift' into this type of work through extension of a contract payroll into word processing for a client. All normal data processing bureau work can be performed including such applications as stock control.

Obviously sales ledger and purchase ledger work will continue to be important but the two large growth areas are financial accounting and management accounting. With general ledger work, accounting information can be produced by cost centre, by product and by other variables. An analysis of variances against budget is also a useful service (and for some clients may be essential).

In the production of management accounts, great attention should be paid to the design of good management information in the routine reports.

From the case studies it can be seen that some accounting firms had special accounting systems to service a particular customer (e.g. a solicitor's package) whilst others concentrated on general purpose accounting systems.

Financial director or consultant role

In addition to the data processing role, accounting firms could design a management accounting system which they would operate. They would then perform the data processing service *and* provide a complete commentary and analysis, thereby undertaking the performance tracking and diagnosis role for the client. We found some evidence (see for example Practices 3 and 4) of accounting firms moving in this direction.

The accounting firm could go even further and play an active role at a higher managerial level which could include advice on strategic planning, based on the processing of the routine transactions information. Both of these functions would attract extra fee income.

This is a significant point. If the accounting firm processes the routine transactions, analyses the variance reports, and recommends remedial action, a natural extension of its activities is to carry out the full role of a financial director. A 'company secretary' role could also be performed.

With the inclusion of the facilities described below, the accounting firm can essentially provide a full, comprehensive and complete accounting, financial and data processing service.

Decision support systems

Although it is debatable whether or not decision support systems fall within the scope of a financial director's functions, this activity represents an area which accounting firms could develop successfully, given the right training. In the very small business, formal decision support systems are of little relevance. However, in the small to medium business, which is characterised by its lack of specialist facilities, the accounting firm can assist by performing the following:

(a) Information retrieval functions based on the client's management information system.
(b) Financial planning/modelling using a computer.

Within the second context there are obviously several alternatives such as:

- A long term 10 year plan.
- A medium-term and more detailed 3 to 5 year plan.
- A detailed 12 monthly short term plan.

The latter is essentially either a control device or a cash flow forecast.

Cash flow forecasting and bank monitoring
With the 12 monthly short term plan, the accounting firm faces two distinct but related alternatives:

1. The production of a feasible short term business plan and the consequent monitoring of that plan on behalf of the firm or some external body (e.g. bankers).
2. The production of a cash flow budget and the subsequent realisation of the need for finance. This could lead to the procurement of the finance (i.e. a money lending agency function) with a subsequent monitoring service for which the accounting firm would be ideally placed (especially if it also performed the data processing operations for the client).

This particular service can vary from occasional advice to a more serious loan procurement and monitoring service. Within the two extremes there is a spectrum of intermediate services.

Other financial models

Other uses of computer-based financial planning aids such as financial models include:

(a) Analyses of performance figures.
(b) Ratio analysis.
(c) Tax planning.
(d) Statistical forecasting.
(e) Optimising models.
(f) Probabilistic models.
(g) Portfolio models.

In general, the accounting firm could offer a wide range of operations research and quantitative tools.

Some experts feel that despite modern spreadsheets and other software packages, the building of financial models is still a skilled task for which the average accountant is unprepared by his current professional training.

Referral and sub-contract work

For those accounting firms who do have the necessary expertise and technology, a new source of fee income could be referral work from those firms that lack one or both of these.

Communication and office facilities

Similarly, an accounting firm with the latest technology could offer to its client a range of general services, including:

- All aspects of data processing, not already dealt with.
- An electronically controlled telephone answering system.
- Communication facilities including computer to computer links, data transmission, and so on.
- Prestel and Teletext type service including the use of new information retrieval software on databanks (which are yet to be created).
- An automatic telex service with memory.
- A data transmission/electronic funds transfer service.
- A facsimile reproduction service.
- A microfiche service, file keeping, record keeping and information-retrieval service.
- A photocopy service.
- A word processing and secretarial service.

Thus the accounting firm could expand its range of services to utilise existing equipment and personnel by offering a complete office service.

IMAP-H

Of course, different accounting firms would tend to emphasise some, but not all, of the above.

CONCLUSIONS

To put the sources of fee income in context, it is quite conceivable* that within ten years, the bulk of the fee income from a practice could be derived from these new sources. The large accounting firms have already perceived this. For the Profession in general, a lack of research and educational activity and of positive developments is becoming apparent. The next chapter makes some recommendations to counter this problem. Although they may be controversial, they do need serious and urgent consideration.

In Chapter 6 it was noted that there were some contradictions between our findings of increasing use of microcomputers in small businesses and the conclusion that the bulk of a practice's fee income may be derived from new sources of a 'computer bureau' type. In reality there is no inconsistency. Small businesses may require microcomputers for a variety of reasons, such as estimating or spreadsheet work, apart from the routine accounting function. A practice offering a bureau service is thus likely to experience *both* an increased demand for bureau services as well as an environment in which more and more clients are becoming computerised. Clients may turn to a bureau service for reasons of convenience or especially when the owner/management of a small business encounters problems with a microcomputer (such as software errors/bugs, mechanical/electronic breakdowns or those arising from lack of knowledge/training/familiarity with the software). The pace of the computer revolution is such that there is no necessary contradiction in existence of a potential market for professional office-based computer bureaus and the increasing use of microcomputers by clients.

All the practices operating a bureau type service in Chapter 6 had also experienced a client base that was increasingly using microcomputers. In fact many of the practices visited found that the operation of an in-house computer by a practice provided the necessary awareness and knowledge to enable the practice to begin moving away from auditing around the computer to auditing through the computer (see Chapter 2).

---

*This was expressed in interviews by many practitioners who were aware of the technological changes.

8
Conclusions

INTRODUCTION

We start from the position that the accounting profession should be at the forefront of the information technology revolution. It should seize the opportunity to help and lead the business community, while at the same time generating new business and fee income.

AREAS OF INTEREST FOR THE PROFESSION

There are four central issues for the Profession:
1. The audit of small businesses and the meaning, level and standard of that audit (see Chapters 2 and 4).
2. The level of expertise with respect to computer knowledge of the ICAEW member (see Chapters 2 to 7).
3. The way in which practices operate their internal administration (see Chapters 5 and 6).
4. The range of services offered by a professional practice to its clients (see Chapters 5 to 7).

First, let us focus on the audit and internal problems of the small business following the introduction of a microcomputer-based system. These do indeed create risks for the Profession.

The risks
There are several clear categories of risk which can be classified into four major types:

1. Continued operation of the business.
2. Owner/manager may try to misrepresent the state of the business or defraud it.
3. Employee fraud.
4. Accidental errors.

The first concerns the on-going operations of the business. If certain minimum clerical and operational controls are not present (such as back-up procedures and security copying) the business may be open to an unacceptable level of exposure. If files are lost and cannot be re-created, the situation is likely to be disastrous. Invariably in small businesses there will be missing documentation and this will limit ability to re-create most of the balances. Another problem is that some transactions will have no visible evidence and without a good audit trail there will be no way of re-creating them. In addition, the volume of work leading to the re-creation of the files may be too great for the firm to carry out.

There is consequently some danger that without physical security and a back-up or re-creation facility a firm may lose its records. This may well endanger the survival of the firm as a going concern, and will certainly render the system difficult if not impossible to audit. Most businesses can survive the loss of production facilities which are usually replaceable. The loss of records and information is much more serious and could be fatal for a company.

The second category, that of owner/manager attempting to circumvent the internal control system, is extremely difficult to prevent. Certainly, good software and a sensible hardware configuration make it more difficult. However senior management can initiate, authorise and, in a small business environment, record and review a fraudulent transaction. Automatic data capture might make such dangers more remote but it will not eliminate them altogether.

The third area is less problematic. An employee may attempt to perpetrate a fraud in one of the following ways:

1. Negotiable instrument and forged input frauds.
2. Personal account manipulations such as:
    (a) Account of a 'defrauding' employee.
    (b) Fictitious or unauthorised accounts.
    (c) Account of an unwilling customer or supplier.
    (d) Account of an outside accomplice of a 'defrauding' employee.
    (e) Accomplice of the 'defrauding' employee.

The first can be prevented and/or detected by closely reviewing all cash disbursements. This should be practical in a small business. Even where there are a large number of suppliers and expenses, the number of cheques paid monthly should be small enough for review*.

The type of personal account manipulations which may occur on the sales ledger include:

---

*This section draws upon Chambers (1981).

1. Unauthorised master file amendments which result in lower prices to the accomplice of an employee.
2. An authorised program routine which ensures that the accomplice of an employee is charged the most favourable prices on the computer prices file.
3. A high incidence of credits other than cash (such as credit notes or journal adjustments).
4. Altered credit limits.
5. Doctored transaction data which is rejected by the computer, allowing it to be processed fraudulently by whoever is responsible for making corrections to rejections (this supports the case for segregating the preparation and submission of input from the handling of rejections and resubmissions).
6. Improper write-offs.

Good software, programmed procedures, and audit trail facilities would help to prevent the frauds occurring. By subsequent review the frauds should be capable of detection.

Finally, accidental errors are not usually given the prominence that they deserve, perhaps because fraud is more sensational and therefore news-worthy. Nevertheless, the prevention of accidental errors is important. Errors tend to occur as a result of misclassification, miscalculation or loss of data. They are minimised by good training of personnel and familiarisation with procedures. Within the computing environment, errors can be greatly minimised by the use of good validation techniques which can easily be built into software (assuming that the software is capable of accurately processing data once it is received). Existing good quality software will already incorporate such features and as such they represent a measure of quality.

Examples of validation techniques are:

Date validation.
Account number validation.
Product code validation.
Batch totals.
Hash totals.
Check digits.
Automatic checking of extensions, VAT calculations etc.
Maximum and minimum limits for data.
Range checks.
Missing data check.
Numeric or alphabetic data check.

As with all controls, a balance has to be decided between the degree of control and the ease of access and use of the system. However, with judicious use of some of these controls a very high percentage of accidental errors can be eliminated.

Approaches

In Chapter 2 several alternative approaches to the audit of a small business were examined. They include:

1. A practice audits a small business system by 'auditing around the computer'.
2. A practice may qualify the audit of a small business system, rather than becoming involved in the small business machine.
3. A practice may attempt to carry out a systems-based audit.
4. The Profession may adopt a more radical approach by changing the auditing requirement of a small business, for example, instead of an 'audit' a lower level of certification may be given such as a 'review'.
5. A novel approach is for the practice to offer what is essentially an electronic data processing bureau service and undertake the processing of clients' accounts.
6. The reprocessing by the auditor of the complete transactions/events files generated by the client's system is a promising development.

Approach 4 requires a legal change and would necessitate Government support for such a legislation. Approach 1 has many weaknesses which are discussed in Chapter 2. Approach 2 requires action by the partners in a practice and is in any case only a partial solution. Approach 3 will become more widespread but is dependent on the knowledge and skills of practitioners. Approach 6 is in essence almost in existence in acceptable form. The next few years may see the development of acceptable and commercially available systems.

RECOMMENDATIONS TO THE PROFESSION

1. Internal control

Earlier a number of new solutions were proposed using new innovative approaches. We propose that existing internal control be improved and that new HARDWARE, SOFTWARE and APPLICATIONS SOFTWARE be investigated in order to increase control.

Additionally, the small practice must become more actively involved in the design and installation of small business systems. Central to this idea is the creation of better hardware and software solutions based on existing technology. In the past, small businesses have been difficult to control. With sensible hardware and software solutions we believe it is possible to introduce a higher degree of control in an area which has always had control problems.

As well as sensible hardware and software solutions, the small business using a microcomputer should be provided with an office procedure manual and there should be a basic level of clerical discipline. This would include:

(a) The routine manual filing of source documents in a manner which would allow their easy access.
(b) The retention of all transactions listings, audit trail and routine print-outs in a systematic way.
(c) The taking of security copies of all files.

Sensible hardware solutions include the logging of all transactions and file changes on *either* a hard copy *or* some easily read magnetic medium. The system should have adequate discs and back-up facilities. There should be an element of redundancy with the file store.

Sensible software solutions include some of the following facilities:

• Inability to run source programs.
• Transaction logging and creation of good audit trail.
• Segregation of functions by means of menus with password/security lock protection.
• Recording the opening balance, changes to a balance and closing balance of any account.
• Enforcing the back-up procedures.
• Enforcing the printing of information.
• Making procedures as automatic as possible.
• Building in as many programmed procedures as possible.

Software contamination should be prevented at all costs. This coupled with the maximum of editing/validation/descriptive read-back and redundancy checks should ensure that only clean data enters the system. All entries to the system should be logged. Any file changes should also be logged. The logs and audit trails should be printed daily. Security copies should be enforced.

To the user, it should be emphasised that the machine is not a toy. As with a truck, certain routine maintenance (for example the brakes) would be necessary at any cost. Similarly the business microcomputer should have certain maintenance and clerical routines associated with it. Everyone associates a cash register with tight security. The same attitude should be adopted toward the business microcomputer. If the owner of a business wishes to buy a micro to play with, the toy/leisure article should be separated from the machine used in business. Like a safe, the business computer should be kept secure. (We recognise that this may be a difficult attitude to inculcate especially if the business machine is used as a decision support aid, nevertheless we feel our recommendations should stand).

Finally, an events accounting system has positive control and ease-of-audit advantages. A full event accounting system implies storing all the information surrounding an event in a modern database. Successive parts of the database would then be necessary to produce routine reports or account balances normally held in an accounting system. However a move towards an events accounting system is the retention of the transactions file within a computerised accounting system. Micro-computer based packages using a variation of this concept are already in commercial use. For the control and audit advantages to be fully realised, there should be no possibility of deleting or altering a record on the transaction file (without a suitable entry to that effect on the file) and such facilities are normally not found on existing commercial packages. More evaluation is required to explain the structure and relative advantages of transaction orientated accounting systems.

Working implementations of full events accounting are not yet available and the commercial packages that meet some of the requirements of events accounting have not exploited the control advantages of their systems. However, concern with transactions and their retention (for a year or more) by some businesses would be a useful addition for control purposes. Even if all transactions cannot be retained, the retention of cash disbursements, aggregate transaction types by month, changes to all standing data and so on, may be useful. Emphasis on management action ensures the completeness and accuracy of events is a useful discipline in any case, but it can also make any future transition to events accounting much easier.

There are four possible ways to achieve better internal controls built into the software of current or future computerised systems.

1. A report on the system by a larger accounting firm, with its greater expertise, on behalf of the smaller practice. However, larger firms would be reluctant to put their names to such a report on the grounds of legal liability.

2. 'Review' by computer or accounting companies. This represents a less stringent test than a report with no legal liability (if this can be achieved).

3. Examination or review by a professional body (for example a committee of the Institute), although we recognise that the Institute is

reluctant to take on a time-consuming task with the associated problems already mentioned in 1.

4. Examination or review by the small to medium sized practice (but these firms are likely to have insufficient expertise and will have to buy in or train staff).

2. Auditing

Whether auditing is through or around the computer, the computer system must be examined. This will involve one of three possible methods.

1. The development of new expertise in-house.
2. Referral to another accounting firm with the necessary expertise.
3. Sub-contract to a computer or software company.

Auditing around the computer must involve a more thorough analysis of the computer itself to prevent the risks identified earlier.

However, the design of sensible software and hardware configurations with a certain minimum of office discipline could allow the greater use of systems-based auditing.

The systems-based audit will follow conventional procedures for computer auditing. Internal controls to be identified include:

1. Safeguards against program contamination.
2. Physical security and back-up procedures.
3. Retention of source documents and computer printouts.
4. Programmed procedures.
5. Segregation of function by menus.

(These internal controls are covered in Chapter 4 and Appendix 5.)

As with any control system, strengths in some areas can compensate for weaknesses in other areas.

Compliance testing can take the form of testing the system by means of test data. (For a further discussion of test data see Appendix 3). The function of the auditor would be to test (4) and (5) directly (by test data) and to monitor the extent and type of transactions log and audit trail that is produced by the system. The auditor may also wish to see evidence that suitable physical security, security copies and back-up procedures were in force.

Program contamination could be checked by:

(a) Testing to see whether the operating system allows the compilation of source programs.
(b) Looking at the creation and revision date of the executable code if the operating system has such a facility.

(c) Program source comparison packages (see Appendix 3).

Earlier we talked about management involvement. This type of control technique would be crucial to the audit. If management showed a close interest and knowledge of all customers, suppliers, employees and could explain a sample of transactions then this control could be relied upon even if many of the other controls were weak.

Prior to determining management involvement, there would need to be an element of substantive tests through the use of a computer audit package. (For a further discussion see Appendix 3.) Such a package would graph the number and value of accounts in the sales ledger, purchase ledger and payroll files. Dramatic changes in any general ledger accounts over previous periods would be highlighted. To perform this part of the test satisfactorily it would be useful to have up, say, to five years of comparative data on the general ledger*.

The audit trail in conjunction with the computer audit package must be sufficiently powerful to ascertain all the data relating to or helping to form a particular account balance. Similarly the package must be able to group transactions into particular types and stratify by date and/or value.

Such a package would be helpful in identifying certain transactions which require management explanation.

The use of computer audit extraction packages becomes even more important if one moves towards an events accounting system. Here the requirement could be for a relational query language (e.g. very high level languages often associated with databases – see Chapter 5) with arithmetical and statistical properties. For a further discussion see Moore (1981) and Bhaskar (1984).

3. Training
To audit a small business system requires the knowledge and expertise of computers and business systems. We have already commented that a microcomputer-based system uses some of the advanced features of larger systems (such as on-line/real-time, databases and telecom-munications). Undertaking work in a microcomputer environment

---

*During the course of this work, we developed an experimental computer audit package that can be used under the operating system CP/M. The purpose of developing such a system was to prove that this was possible within the confines of a microcomputer and also to identify the problems, pitfalls and limitations of so doing. With the knowledge and wisdom of developing this system, a better and more efficient commercial system could be developed. However, from the development undertaken, we proved that a generalised computer audit package could be developed for a microcomputer.

requires just as much specialisation as is the case with mainframes, although with a different orientation.

With larger systems, internal control can rely upon batch totals with separate balancing and segregation of duties. In a small business system, the computer itself carries more responsibility for internal control. Consequently, the auditor – if he is to rely on those controls – must be more aware of the computer and its operations than is the case with larger systems.

The view has been expressed that it is uneconomic to audit through the computer of a small business with inexperienced auditors. A sensible hardware and software system will still allow the vouching and audit trail approach of auditing around the system. However it is precisely the small business environment which may not have all the source documents which would aid the vouching approach. Auditing through the computer may therefore permit a higher degree of audit comfort for a small business, especially one where accounts may have been qualified previously.

The training implications are twofold:

1. A greater degree of computer knowledge is necessary if an evaluation of a small business system is to take place.
2. For an efficient audit, the auditor will be required to test the system and carry out substantive work on the computer using a file inter-rogation technique.

In addition the small practice will also be the natural place for a small business to turn to for advice concerning computers. Areas where help is required, particularly if the client is a first time user, are:

(a) Advice and help in selection of a small computer.
(b) Systems analysis, design and specification of applications software.
(c) Implementation of the system.
(d) Acceptance testing.
(e) Advice on security and efficiency of processing and the quality of management information emerging.
(f) Evaluation and recommendations as to internal control.
(g) Documentation and manuals.
(h) Office procedures around (including input and output from) the computer.

The training implications are thus very great indeed.

The Institute runs a number of informative courses which members wishing to increase their knowledge should attend. Useful experience can also be gained by a practice learning from the adoption of a computer to aid its own administration.

OBSERVATIONS

Appendix 1 lists some recommendations which we thought appropriate when writing this report. It is to the credit of the Institute that action has already been taken on many of these issues.

One problem we foresee is that members are currently expending too much money and effort on computerisation. Whilst there are educational benefits from this learning curve, there is also an element of wasteful duplication. Almost all the case studies considered in Chapter 6 who had computerised an element of their office procedures were involved in the development or refinement of the software. This amounted to a great deal of development and implementation effort which is being duplicated simultaneously in different practices. They are 're-inventing the wheel' in parallel.

It could be argued that this duplication is a justified form of competition. However, the process of duplication is expensive and results in higher costs for the profession as a whole. We do not believe that the amount of duplication currently found is in the best interests of the Profession nor, in particular, of the provision of a cost effective service to clients.

Finally, at some point the Institute must decide how active and assertive it wants to be and to what extent it wants to aid the majority of its members rather than the larger firms who already have the necessary specialist staff.

APPENDIX 1

Policy recommendations

INTRODUCTION

There are several avenues in which further research is needed:

1. Research should be be initiated into the meaning of the term 'audit' within a small business context. Audit is a matter of evidence and the audit opinion is concerned with the adequacy of the evidence. Within the context of a small business it is more difficult to get this evidence. In fact it is a feature of the small business that audit evidence is less than in large firms. Three possibilities arise:
    (a) Expand the scope of the small audit qualification and issue some rules and regulations governing its use.
    (b) Make the value of the audit some function of the size of the firm and/or the degree of audit evidence.
    (c) Replace 'audit' by some other term with a lower level of integrity attached to it.
2. Research should be conducted into the nature of secure hardware, software and applications software using state of the art technology. Sensible hardware using existing technology with a good operating system and well-designed and developed applications software, can provide an improved degree of internal control for a small business. There is a strong possibility of dramatically improving internal control; thereby making the small business subject to a degree of control never before established.

    Research should be encouraged into:
    (a) Hardware configurations.
    (b) Operating systems software and the limitation of general purpose facilities; that is, including a comprehensive password system, but with no facility to edit and recompile a program and no facility to edit data other than through an authorised applications program.

(c) Well-written and robust software. with good internal controls built in, good audit trail and enforced menu-separation of the traditional segregation of function roles.

3. Research should be sponsored into the use of events accounting systems.

4. The Institute may like to consider the two conflicting views. One is that the Professsion or the Institute should undertake a more assertive role by:

    (a) Developing the applications software itself.

    (b) Giving guidelines as to hardware, software and applications.

    (c) Certifying or approving existing systems.

    All three ideas would lead to better standards of control for small business machines. The Institute is already acting to achieve b. (Sherwood 1983-4). We believe that further research is required into the possibility of the Institute carrying out c.

    The opposing view is that, using the medical profession as an example, this would be analogous to asking the Royal College of Surgeons to dictate the use of a particular brand of operating instruments.

5. Research is needed into training needs and the syllabus of the ICAEW and other professional bodies' examinations.

    Requirements include:

    - More training which is examinable.
    - More practical experience.
    - Some 'hands on' supervised computer auditing and evaluation of internal controls.

    The role of training, syllabus and work experience, we believe, must be fundamentally re-thought in the light of the new and rapidly changing technology.

6. Research needs to be carried out into the ethical problems surrounding the expansion of the Profession into new chargeable computer-based activities. We believe that these activities and the consequent need for new ways of ensuring minimal ethical standards must be researched and investigated. Compatibility and consistency with the Eighth Directive must also be ensured.

    Although this report envisages that accounting firms will increase their data processing bureau type work, this is not meant to preclude other non-accounting firms from being 'certified' (if indeed this occurs) or from performing bureau work.

7. The Institute must examine ways in which the smaller practice can be given some of the competitive advantage of the larger practice's specialised staff and data processing capabilities. One possibility is

that the Institute should run a powerful database and interrogation facility for small practices. This could be extended into a service bureau to provide a word processing and/or accounts preparation service. In addition, there could be a standard Institute micro-computer.

This would enable the small practice to have access to good soft-ware and to increase the competitiveness of the small practice vis-a-vis the larger firm. The larger firm could have the choice of using the standard Institute product, or developing its own 'superior' product.

Of course, the Institute may decide not to intervene. Any redress of the competitive advantage that accrues to the larger firm which can afford specialisation is ultimately a political question; one which the Institute may not wish to influence.

One of the services the Institute could provide is the Members book (which should be in machine-readable form). This could be provided either by a Prestel-type service or any floppy disc to be used with standard software.

8. If a small practice has insufficient experience or ability, one of three types of organisation can help, either by the previous concept of approving certain systems, or through the process of referral. These organisations for the certification of systems include:
   (a) The Institute itself, either using a specialist taskforce or through the usual committee structure.
   (b) One of the larger accounting firms with the necessary specialism.
   (c) A computer or software house with the necessary accounting knowledge and internal control skills.

Organisations (b) and (c) could carry out work on one-off projects, whilst it is conceivable that the Institute might set up a consultancy division to help the smaller practice. However, the Institute is more likely to be involved in certifying a brand computer system (in-clusive of software).

We understand that the CCAB Computer Liaison Committee in association with the National Computing Centre is exploring these issues. We still believe that the Institute should be more directly involved and should improve its own, rather than some other organi-sation's standards.

All of the above possibilities require investigation and further research.

SUGGESTIONS FOR FUTURE RESEARCH

Collecting together points made previously, the authors believe that it is vital for the Institute to continue with the research which they have initiated. Many research areas have been identified above but little or no research is being carried out in the areas of Policy Recommendations 2 and 3. These are respectively research into:

- The nature of secure hardware, software and applications software using existing technology.
- More advanced categories of hardware, operating systems and applications software including the use of events accounting systems.

SUGGESTIONS FOR CONFERENCES AND OTHER INITIATIVES

Given the observations and conclusions of the report, we would urge the Institute to set up the following:

1. An annual conference dealing with a variety of aspects in computing and covering the broad spectrum of topics from microcomputers in the smaller practice to computer auditing of sophisticated systems.
2. A new course on the auditing of microcomputer systems that slots in below the level of the course 'small computers' (which is primarily aimed at mini- rather than microcomputers).
3. To counter the British Computer Society's attempt to dominate the areas of controls and the audit of computer systems the Institute should consider whether a joint initiative can be launched, involving a committee (working with other bodies similar to the Joint Board of Accreditation). The precise function of this committee needs careful thought. One possibility is for this committee to perform the following functions:
   (a) To liaise with the British Computer Society and other organisations which might have an interest in the control, security or audit of such systems.
   (b) To organise the annual conference mentioned in (1) above.
   (c) To liaise and issue documents and updates (these may be frequent because of the rate of technological progress) concerned with accounting standards in relation to the use of computers.
   (d) To act on the recommendations of the Auditing Practice Committee and produce updates (again these may be frequent because of the rate of technological progress).
   (e) To revise and update the various syllabuses in the Professional examinations, insofar as the rate of technological progress may require constant revision.

Such an initiative would be fully in accordance with the Institute's recently issued (January 1984) Information Technology Policy Statement (Sherwood 1983-4).

APPENDIX 2

Aids for system selection and examples of commercially available small business systems

POPULAR COMPUTERISED APPLICATIONS

1. Time recording.
2. Word processing.
3. Sales, Purchase and Nominal Ledgers.
4. Payroll.
5. Incomplete Records (Accounting Systems) 'In Practice'/'Bureaus'.
6. Accounts preparation:
   With word processing facilities.
   Comparison capabilities.
   Trial balance preparation to final account capabilities.
   Standard formats.
7. Financial modelling.

SOME DECISION CRITERIA FOR SYSTEM SELECTION

1. Suppliers/Manufacturers.
2. Machine.
3. Software.
4. Operating System.

1. *Suppliers/Manufacturers*

History	Support
Prospects	Maintenance
Machines	Location
Software	Size

2. *Machine*
    Manufacturers/Suppliers   Availability
    Capability (Speed etc)   Machine growth capability
    Peripherals   Compatibility
    Storage methods   Operating system
    Prospects   Applications
    History   Cost
    Reliability   Extent of usage

3. *Software*
    History   Capacity requirements
    Capabilities   Operating system
    Tailorability/flexibility   Expandability
    Compatibility   Cost
    Machines   Extent of usage
    Modularity   Suitability

4. *Operating system*
    History   Multi-user/Network
    Ease of use   Compatibility
    Reliability
    Cost

CRITERIA FOR SUPPLIER CHOICE

1. Wide range of systems.
2. Experience of the systems.
3. Demonstration of a knowledge of accounting problems as well as computing.
4. Good support after sale, maintenance and repairs.
5. Ability to offer complete and compatible systems to remove physical set-up and compatibility problems.
6. Satisfied customers.
7. Size and long-term viability of suppliers' organisation.

GENERAL REQUIREMENTS FOR MICRO-SYSTEMS

Sections:
1. Hardware.
2. Packages and software.
3. Languages.
4. Operating systems.
5. User friendliness.

1. *Hardware*

   (a) Capacity to handle large volumes of data.
   (b) Ability to handle increases in this volume in the short term.
   (c) Reliability (relevant to all sections above).
   (d) A proven history of successful operation.

2. *Packages and software*

   (a) Must be a close match to user's requirements.
   (b) Capacity to be tailored/extended to specific needs.
   (c) Reliability/proven history.
   (d) Consistent treatment/good control of accounting conventions and data processing.

3. *Languages*

   (a) Preferably established.
   (b) Short learning horizon (for average user).

4. *Operating systems*

   (a) Preferably established.
   (b) Ease of use.
   (c) Capacity to control peripherals.

5. *User friendliness: (the whole system)*

   (a) Ease of set-up/running procedures.
   (b) Minimal training.
   (c) Minimal installation and implementation time.
   (d) Operating system and packages are the main influence on 'user friendliness' of the system and as such, must be clear, reliable and well-supported by documentation and training.

WHICH COMPUTER?

1. 'Personal' computers.
2. 8-bit computers.
3. 16-bit computers.

1. *'Personal' computers*
   Minimum configuration cost is targeted at the general public, but configurations can be upgraded for small business usage with some

success. They have a low grade entry level cost but are not generally capable of handling large volumes of data.

2. *8-bit computers*
    Microcomputers which contain an 8-bit microprocessor are so called because they store information (data) in blocks of 8 BInary digiTs (0s and 1s) for each character (number, letter and symbol). They differ from personal computers mainly because the business user is less concerned with entry cost. This means increased levels of sophistication, in capacity and capability are available. Established growth paths also exist; for example, increased memory in the form of hard discs for information storage. The 8-bit machine is the most widely used machine at present, but the advent of 16-bit machines may challenge its popularity.

3. *16-bit computers*
    The new generation of micros use 16 binary digits to store characters. Obviously the applications for these machines are still not as prolific as 8-bit applications, but their availability is surely only a matter of time. Similarly, the widespread approval of the operating systems do not exist yet due to the 'relatively small' number of users.

    The advantages of 16-bit over 8-bit machines appear to be greater speed and more capability (16-bit machines have capabilities to support a number of users, with a screen and keyboard).

Overview
Operations can be successfully achieved on configurations costing £5,000 to £6,000 upwards.

Hard discs are available for data storage, increasing capacity, normally to a maximum of about 100 megabytes:

   8 bits equals 1 byte.
   1000 bytes equals 1Kb (1 kilobyte).
   1000 Kb equals 1 Mb (1 megabyte)
   therefore 1 Mb is 1 million bytes (1 million characters).

8-bit machines seem to have a limited development in the future, because 16-bit ones are better and hardware is being made more cheaply. Acceptable software always lags behind hardware enhancement. For example, there are 32-bit machines under development, but little software to run on them.

STORAGE MEDIA

As costs fall, hard discs (which are similar to LP records in appearance, sealed in a dust-proof container) with their greater capacity will become more economic and desirable to the user than the floppy discs presently used in small systems:

Disadvantages of floppy disc compared to hard disc
1. Lower capacity.
2. Sensitive to temperature, humidity, rough handling, etc.
3. Subject to 'data-fade' (loss of data over time and usage etc.).
4. Hard discs are sealed, not handled, and allow faster access to information and more efficient storage.

Advantages of floppy discs
1. Comparatively inexpensive.
2. Modular (e.g. one disc for each application).
3. Easily replaceable/portable.

FUNCTIONS OF AN OPERATING SYSTEM

1. To deal with initial incompatibilities of hardware brands so that applications will operate with different components.
2. To provide a framework to work in; managing resources, storing and retrieving data and files.
3. Give the user control over peripherals (printer, plotter screens, etc.).
4. Assist user by supplying power and flexibility to solve problems.
5. More recent systems provide support for a number of users.

Desirable utilities:
1. Real time or batch operation.
2. Single/multiple user capability – resource sharing.
3. Network capability (Local area networks – LANs).
4. Reliability – crash proof.
5. Easily maintained and updated.
6. Flexible and user friendly.
7. Recovery capability (if system crashes).
8. Good error handling capability.
9. Security (password capabilities, access restrictions).
10. An editor for use by the user.
11. Automatic archiving of superseded files.
12. Automatic time, date and version specification given to files.

13. Automatic start-up procedure.
14. Diagnostic help, information and debugging facilities.
15. Applications available.

COMMERCIALLY AVAILABLE SYSTEMS

Guidance on the scope and extent of such systems may be derived from a number of sources, including currently:

Company Publications Limited
International Directory of Software (published annually) – contains details of over 2,000 software products including some 650 pages of information on accounting and associated software, including many micro systems packages.

Company Publications Limited
Microcomputer Software Directory (published annually with quarterly updates) contains over 80 pages of detail in connection with accounting, management information and business and commercial software packages available on a variety of microcomputers, and references to relevant suppliers.

Macmillan Press Limited
The Ultimate Software Selector (1984) – contains extensive details of over 1000 micro business software packages, and references to relevant suppliers.

NCC Limited
Directory of Software Packages and Suppliers (updated monthly).

Accountants Digest
Accountants Digest No. 121
'Choosing a microcomputer for the smaller company' by J A Oxley, ICAEW, Summer 1982.
Accountants Digest No. 131
'Audit of small computers' by C C Malcolm and W J A Meadows, ICAEW, Spring 1983.
Accountants Digest No. 139
'Computers for the practising accountant' by C T Edge, ICAEW, Summer 1983.
Accountants Digest No. 153
'Financial modelling' by Dennis Sherwood, ICAEW, Winter 1983/84.

APPENDIX 3

CAATS-considered: a practical view of computer assisted audit techniques*

ROD PERRY
(Coopers and Lybrand)

INTRODUCTION

The purpose of this Appendix is to consider the better known techniques for auditing in a computer environment. Not all of these techniques necessarily require direct use of the computer but tend to be loosely termed computer assisted audit techniques (CAATS) because they relate to tests of programs or files. This section seeks to establish for the auditor, who is under constant pressure to select the most efficient way to carry out his audit, the practical aspects of individual techniques, the potential benefits of each technique and the audit relevance. The views expressed are my own, as much of the analysis of the techniques is necessarily subjective.

THE MORE COMMON TECHNIQUES

The more common techniques have been set out in Table A3.1 together with a brief explanation of what they are and some comments on their

---

*This paper was first presented at the ICAEW conference of 1983. Although there have been some technical changes in CAATS since it was written, it remains an authoritative introduction to the subject.

practical advantages and disadvantages. Broadly speaking each of the techniques may be classified as being primarily a technique for:

- Systems testing.
- Validation of data.
- Testing of integrity controls (also known as 'general controls' or 'organisational controls').

Table A3.1 The most common computer assisted audit techniques

Techniques	Description	Advantages	Disadvantages
Interrogation audit software	Software used by the auditor to read data on client's files and provide information for the audit	• Performs wide variety of audit tasks. • Long term economies • Reads actual records • Capable of dealing with huge volumes	• Requires a degree of skill to use • Initial set up costs can be high • Adaptation needed from machine to machine
Parallel simulation	Software used by the auditor to re-perform procedures carried out by client's programs	• Performs wide variety of audit tasks • Long term economies • Capable of dealing with huge volumes	• Requires a degree of skill to use • Initial set up costs can be high • Adaptation needed from machine to machine
Log analysers	Software used by the auditor to read and analyse records of machine activity	• Provides a high degree of information on machine usage • Long term economies • Effective when testing integrity controls	• Requires a high degree of skill to use and to action the reports • Limited availability as regards machine types • High volume of records restricts extent of test

Techniques	Description	Advantages	Disadvantages
Database analysers	Software used by the auditor to examine the rights associated with terminals and the ability of users to access information on a database	• Provides a lot of information concerning the operation of the database • Gets the auditor involved with the database management system	• Requires a high degree of skill to set up and to action the reports • Restricted availability both as regards machine types and database management systems • Specific and limited audit applicability
Program library analysers	Software used by the auditor to examine dates of changes made to the load library and the use of utilities to amend programs	• Provides the auditor with useful information concerning the program library • Identifies abnormal changes to the library • Useful when testing program security for data processing installations	• Requires a high degree of skill to use and follow up reports • Availability restricted to certain machine types • Only relevant when testing integrity controls
Core image comparison	Software used by the auditor to compare the load version of a program against a secure master copy	• Provides a high degree of comfort concerning the load version of the program • Particularly useful where only load versions are distributed	• Requires a high degree of skill to set up and interpret the results • Where programs have been re-compiled the comparison may be invalidated as the program records everything as a difference

Techniques	Description	Advantages	Disadvantages
			• Printouts are hard to interpret and the actual changes made difficult to establish • Availability restricted to certain machine types
Source comparison	Software used by the auditor to examine the source version of a program against a secure master copy	• Compares source code line by line and identifies all differences • Useful when testing integrity controls or particularly important program procedures	• Other procedures are necessary to be satisfied that the executable version reflects the source code examined • Requires a fair degree of skill to use and interpret the results • Availability restricted to certain machine types
Test data – live, dead or integrated test facility	Fictitious data applied against the client's programs either whilst they are running or in an entirely separate operation. The results of processing the fictitious data are compared with the expected results based on the auditor's understanding of the programs involved	• Performs a wide variety of tasks • Gives considerable comfort about the operation of programs • Can be precisely targetted for specific procedures within programs • Long term economies	• Dead test data requires additional work for the auditor to satisfy himself the right programs were used • Live test data can have unfortunate side effects • Technique can be expensive to set up and cumbersome to use

Techniques	Description	Advantages	Disadvantages
			• Adequate for detection of major error but less likely to detect deep-seated fraud
Manual simulation screen testing	Techniques whereby the auditor arranges or manipulates data either real or fictitious, in order to see that a specific program or screen edit test is doing its work	• Very widely applicable • Easy to use, requiring little dp skill • Can be targetted for specific functions carried out by programs	• Each use merely does one particular objective • Can create unexpected side effects
Program code analysis	An examination by the auditor of the source code of a particular program with a view to following the logic of the program so as to satisfy himself that it will perform according to his understanding	• Gives a reasonable degree of comfort of the logic of the program concerned • The auditor can examine the totality of the program code	• The auditor must understand the program language • Auditor needs to check that the source code represents the version on the source library, and that the version equates to the executable version
Embedded code	Software used by the auditor to examine transactions passing through the system by placing his own program in the suite of programs used for processing	• Performs wide variety of audit tasks • Examines each transaction as it passes through the system • A form of continuous auditing • Capable of identifying unusual transactions passing through the system	• There is a processing overhead involved because of the extra programs • Definition of what constitutes an unusual transaction needs to be very precise • Precautions need to be taken over the output file from the programs, so as to ensure its security

Techniques	Description	Advantages	Disadvantages
			• Precautions need be taken to ensure that the program cannot be suppressed or tampered with
Tracing	Software used by the auditor to identify which instructions were used in a program and in what order	• Helps to analyse the way in which a program operates	• There are cheaper ways to achieve the same objective, although not perhaps in the same detail • Requires a high degree of skill to use and interpret • Adaptation needed from machine to machine
Mapping	Software used by the auditor to list unused program instructions	• Identifies unutilised program code which may be there for fraudulent reasons	• Very specific objective • Requires a high degree of skill to use and interpret the results • Adaptation needed from machine to machine
Modelling	A variety of software, usually associated with a microcomputer, enabling the auditor to carry out analytical reviews of client's results, to alter conditions so as to identify	• Can be very powerful analytical tools • Can enable the auditor to examine provisions on a number of different bases • Very flexible	• The auditor requires access to a microcomputer or other machine • Results require careful interpretation • High degree of auditing skill required

Techniques	Description	Advantages	Disadvantages
	amounts for provisions or claims, or to project results and compare actual results with those expected	in use • Can provide the auditor with useful information on trends and patterns	• Limited amount of software currently available
Snapshots	Software used by the auditor to take a picture of a file of data or a transaction passing through the system at a particular point in time	• Permits the auditor to freeze processing at a point in time to carry out tests, or to confirm the way a particular aspect of the system operates	• Can be expensive to set up • Fairly limited and specific audit objectives

The auditor makes use of CAATS for either of the following two reasons:

- It will provide, short term or long term, the most efficient way for him to carry out the tests.
- It is the only practical way that a test or series of tests which are deemed to be necessary, can be carried out.

CAATS are used either because the auditor has decided that he must validate certain data held on computer files, or passing through the system, and that the best way to achieve this is to obtain his own independent printout; or because he has decided to rely on aspects of the computer systems. Where he chooses to rely on the system he will need to satisfy himself that the important programs involved are functioning properly. This will require that he either tests directly the relevant procedures within the programs or that he tests the controls in the data processing centre which guarantee the integrity of the programs and data files. In either case, because of the nature of the work, he is likely to require CAATS in order to assist him with the tests.

Consider the following three situations:

- A company with a medium sized computer, where the main applications are computerised but have indifferent internal controls. The auditor will be unable to place full reliance on the systems and will lean towards use of software to help him validate the data on the computer files.

- A similar company but one which has a good system of internal control. Here the auditor may well choose to rely on the systems of internal control but may find that the integrity controls are not strong enough for him to place a great deal of reliance upon them. In this case if he wishes to rely on the systems to limit his validation work he will need to test the critical programmed procedures and will need to determine the most effective way to do this. This is likely to involve the use of CAATS. In addition, he might augment the system tests by selective software in his validation work.

- A major company having a large and well run computer department, extensive use of terminals with on-line systems to remote branches; and a high volume of transactions. The auditor is likely to wish to rely on systems and might well wish to carry out tests of the integrity controls within the computer department. He would be likely to make extensive use of software both to help in his systems work and in his validation tests. Other CAATS might be required to test the integrity controls and in some parts of the systems testing.

NATURE OF CAATS

CAATS vary widely in the extent of their use and in the degree of satisfaction which each individual technique can provide. Some are very general in that they can be used in a variety of ways and achieve a number of different audit objectives. Software is notable in this respect. Other techniques are more specific, in that the technique is designed to meet one particular objective in the audit process; for example, manual simulation or program code analysis, although they can be used in a variety of different audit situations, i.e. their applicability is wide but their objective is narrow.

Some of the other techniques are only relevant if the auditor intends to rely upon integrity controls and indeed many of these techniques are limited still further by being restricted to particular mainframes. The remaining techniques tend to be very specific. The auditor would only consider their use where he has a particular purpose in mind or a particular system which can only be audited effectively by the choice of exactly the right technique. Generally speaking, techniques falling into this category might be database analysers and tracing and mapping.

Broadly speaking, those techniques which utilise software, e.g. audit software, source compare, log analysers etc, are machine specific although there may be separate versions which can be run on different machines. The auditor would require the right version for the right machine. Other techniques tend to be machine independent, for example test data, manual simulation, program code analysis etc.

Because the auditor must provide the most effective and economic service to his clients, he has to have knowledge of all the techniques so as to provide him with a full range of options. However, it is worth noting that usage of some of the more esoteric techniques continues to be minimal.

DOCUMENTATION REQUIRED FOR CAATS

As for any other audit test, the auditor will need to retain sufficient documentation on the audit file to provide evidence of the tests carried out, the levels and the conclusions drawn. However, in the case of most CAATS the auditor is likely to require to use them again in subsequent years. He will therefore need to keep additional documentation on the particular technique such that he is able to re-run the technique for future audits. The nature of this documentation will vary according to the technique but the principles which are applied to documentation of audit software can be usefully applied to the other techniques.

ADVANTAGES AND DISADVANTAGES OF THE TECHNIQUES

The various techniques are analysed below in Table A3.2 in a number of ways:

- An indication of whether they are fundamentally single or multi objective techniques.
- An indication of the amount of time required for use in the first year. It should be recognised that for many of the techniques, the efficiencies are only realised in second and subsequent years, when runtimes become minimal but powerful audit objectives can be achieved. This applies particularly to audit software and test data.
- An assessment of the degree of skill required to use the technique.
- A subjective view of the degree of audit satisfaction which can be obtained from each technique. It must be recognised that the audit satisfaction obtained will vary considerably according to the circumstances in which the technique is used. Indeed, some techniques are dependent on the audit strategy adopted, e.g. integrity control techniques.

Some idea of the extent of use of the different techniques based on an

Table A3.2 Computer assisted audit techniques

	Category of use	Single or multi objective	Degree of applicability	Machine availability	Usage	Time required	DP skill level	Degree of audit satisfaction
Interrogation software	V	M	W	M	E	C-S	R-C	C
Parallel simulation	S	S	R	M	R	C-S	C	C
Log analysers	I	M	S	F	M	C-R	C	C
Database analysers	S	M	S	F	M	C-R	C	S
Program library analysers	I	S	S	F	M	C-R	C	R
Core image comparison	S/I	S	S	F	M	R	C	S
Source comparison	S/I	S	R	S	R	R	C	S
Test data, (live, dead or ITF)	S	M	W	I	R	C-S	R	C
Manual simulation	S	S	W	I	E	S	S	S
Program code analysis	S	S	R	I	R	R	C	S
Embedded code	V	M	W	M	R	C-R	C	C
Tracing and mapping	S	S	S	F	M	R	C	S
Snapshots	S	S	S	F	M	R	C	S
Modelling	V	M	W	I	M-E	R	S-R	C

S = Systems S = Single W = Wide F = Few E = Extensive (C = Considerable)
V = Validation M = Multi R = Reasonable S = Some R = Regular (R = Reasonable)
I = Integrity S = Specific M = Most M = Minimal (S = Small)
    controls I = Independent

informal survey within the largest accounting firms is shown in Table A3.3.

Table A3.3 Big 8 – informal survey of use.

	Extensive	Regular	Minimal	None
Interrogation software	8			
Log analysers		1	3	4
Data base analysers		2	2	3
Program library analysers			4	4
Core image comparison			2	6
Source comparison		2	3	3
Test data		5	2	1
Program code analysis		1	6	1
Embedded code		3	2	3
Tracing and mapping				8
Modelling	3	1	1	3

Extensive = More than 20 uses per year   Minimal = Less than 5 uses per year
Regular = Between 5 and 20 uses per year   None = No regular audit usage

CONCLUSIONS FROM ANALYSIS

It is always attractive to identify particular products as 'a best buy'. However, this is inevitably simplistic as it fails to take account of the different circumstances which will pertain to each client. Having said this, one might conclude as follows:

Audit software
This technique is now well established and widely used. Potentially it is of such benefit that its use should always be considered where records are maintained on computer files. Considerable effort and expense has been put into the development of audit software over the last decade, so as to provide ever more efficient ways of interrogating data files and reperforming client results. Its wide use across the spectrum of the profession is a practical demonstration of the range of objectives that can be achieved, its ability to examine the data files themselves, its flexibility and its ultimate economy.

Modelling techniques, including normative auditing and analytical review tools using microcomputers are expanding rapidly. Currently, there is considerable use of such software within many professional firms and the use is likely to increase rapidly as auditors become more familiar with the technique and as more software becomes available. A considerable effort is likely to be made in this sphere of activity in the short term.

Manual simulation and screen testing
Wherever auditors do systems-based auditing and need to reperform programmed procedures, these techniques are likely to be high on the list. Most of these tests can be carried out manually and require little computer expertise. The nature, level and spread of tests vary widely from client to client.

Log and program library analysers
Both of these techniques can be very useful where integrity controls are being tested. Their use is currently limited because of the restrictions on machine type and the relatively small number of audits where this approach currently appears to be preferred.

Test data
In whatever guise test data is used, it remains a useful tool for particular circumstances. In many cases tests which might be carried out by test data can equally be carried out by audit software, the latter being frequently preferred. There will always be certain conditions where test data remains the appropriate test but its use is likely to be fairly limited.

Embedded code
The technique is most useful in certain types of audit. It can be particularly relevant where the auditor is relying upon a statistical sample of transactions which are to be validated. It is not a very prevalent technique because it requires considerable set-up effort, there is a processing overhead involved as all the transactions have to pass through the embedded code, and it is often difficult to establish the requisite degree of independence. It is, however, quite popular with internal auditors.

Program code analysis
A technique which tends to be used only in specific circumstances, where the auditor requires to test a particularly critical program. It is restricted in its objectives. Considerable technical skill is required to use it. Further, the auditor has still only examined source code and not the executable version.

Source comparison and core image comparison programs
The former tend to be used more frequently than the latter because the software itself is much more satisfactory. However, the audit objectives of source comparison are often limited and can in themselves be ineffective without the use of core image comparison, which looks at the executable version.

Core image comparison is restricted by machine type and has a tendency to be difficult to interpret where the versions being compared are not the same, or even where they have been compiled at different times.

Database analyser
This is a useful but very specific testing medium. It often aids understanding of the system rather than testing the system. Analysers are machine and database specific and therefore of limited availability.

Tracing, mapping and snap shots
Although these techniques are used in particular circumstances from time to time, their use is likely to remain peripheral.

FUTURE PROSPECTS

It is perhaps surprising how little change has taken place in the number and variety of techniques which the auditor has used since the report produced by the Stanford Research Institute in 1977. It is possibly a reflection of the fact that the technology has tended towards continued improvement over the last decade rather than dramatic change. In addition it should be remembered that the extent of use of CAATS, particularly of software, has risen enormously. Nevertheless, there are current changes in technology which could influence the use of individual techniques and make the invention of new techniques more likely.

Microcomputers
The audit use of microcomputers is expanding rapidly. They provide the opportunity to collect data from clients' machines, to manipulate that data and to use modelling techniques and analytical review tools; there are a host of other possibilities. This is likely to be the biggest single area of change in the short term.

Growth of distributed systems
Depending upon how distributed systems are ultimately controlled, increase use might lead to a change of emphasis within the application of

certain techniques; for example, embedded code might become more attractive and core image comparisons more realistic.

Communications
Communications are likely to become more important in computer systems, in both local and wider networks. It is likely that we shall need to develop new techniques to deal with communications, possibly incorporating the trapping of transactions through the telephone network, as some have suggested, which is itself a form of embedded code.

Increasing use of security software
More and more systems are relying upon security software to restrict access to the system. We are likely to need programs to interrogate password tables (if this is not itself a breach of security) and to inspect data dictionaries.

Manufacturers' packages, report generators and expert systems
These are all likely to become more commonplace. This may change the way in which auditors use software and by making software easier to run make the technique more widely available.

Data capture techniques
Input techniques are likely to change rapidly. Voice input will gradually come into being, although it is likely to be a long time before it is commonplace in accounting systems. There will be an increasing absence of hard copy and a continued trend towards the pushing of data capture back to the user. Each of these will require a fresh approach and a reconsideration of techniques by the auditor.

In addition, audit firms are likely to put considerable effort into the development of better and more extensive audit software, including the use of application-specific packages and ever more efficient generalised file interrogation software. Developments in software for the microcomputer will continue rapidly. It is likely that a greater emphasis on integrity controls will lead to the development of more audit skills and techniques to assist in this area of work.

APPENDIX 4

Implications for audit approaches

From a review of the literature, empirical observation and opinions given by accounting firms, it is evident that there are two basic practical approaches to the auditing of small computer based systems using systems based auditing techniques. In addition, a third theoretical approach may also be considered.

The first two practical approaches are similar but adopt slightly different methodologies and procedures.

APPROACH A

In compliance testing, one line of investigation is an examination of the extent to which user controls can be relied upon (e.g. control totals). If they prove unreliable, then programmed procedures may compensate for the lack of user controls as long as reliance can be placed on computer controls.

The problem with this approach is that few microcomputer systems will pass the various stages in which decisions have to be taken. Ultimately, the use of computer assisted audit techniques is required to test the validity of programmed procedures and to carry out some substantive work. This approach is further discussed at the end of this appendix.

APPROACH B

Whilst following the same pattern as approach A, this approach assumes that there can be no general reliance on controls for audit purposes. The starting point is to find any user controls or programmed procedures upon which reliance may be placed. Where a control can be relied upon, the audit environment is then examined (perhaps just for that application) and compliance tests carried out.

The extent to which compliance tests are used depends on the weakness of the disciplines surrounding the controls; the reliance on compliance tests and the reduction in substantive tests cannot be as great as the reduction possible in a controlled environment.

Approaches A and B are less relevant when there is a complete absence of general computer controls and of disciplines surrounding some controls. The next approach is probably the best one for dealing with such a business environment. This approach is also further discussed at the end of this appendix.

A NEW APPROACH

This approach involves the use of new combinations of hardware and software. Integrity in the system would be preserved by means of the following special features:

1. The applications software would be purchased with the machine, which would then be unable to compile programs or run anything except executable code, written into the firmware of the micro-computer and not transferable to another system.
2. Programs could not be deleted or added to the system without specialist engineering advice. General utility facilities such as an edit device would not be available.
3. No changes could be made to any data file other than through a program which would retain details of that change and auto-matically create a hard copy as evidence of that change.
4. The applications software would be of a high standard.

In general the solution would be to ensure that there are as many programmed procedures as possible. To be able to rely on the integrity of such controls, we must be in a position to say that:

1. The system has not changed.
2. The programmed procedures are strong.
3. The audit trail is either stored in full or printed without fail.

If the audit trail is stored then it is vital that no one is able to change the data without a record of its change (see Weber (1982)).

User controls and disciplines over controls would be weak, but the general controls compensate for this because the programmed procedures and the full audit trail which is created, are sufficiently reliable. This strategy would require the adoption of conventional computer audit techniques, but would demand good software.

The computer audit would concentrate on the following areas:

(a) The programmed procedures would be relied upon to a great extent. This is necessary if the auditor is to test the software.

(b) For (a) to be relied upon, the integrity of the software must be ascertained. The auditor would have to confirm that there was no possibility of program contamination. An examination of the files and operating system to ensure that there are no compilation facilities or evidence of compilation may provide some audit comfort, as would the creation date (if found) of the programs.

(c) The integrity of the data files must also be ascertained. It is important to prevent the processing of files on another computer system where program contamination may be possible.

(d) Verification of the non-visible evidence on the computer through file interrogation techniques.

One of the principal features of a good system would be to provide a good audit trail for both transactions and changes to standing data. Some auditors may be able to use file interrogation techniques on a file which would permanently store the audit trail or transactions (see Weber (1982)).

We have already discussed some of the principles behind good software in Alternative 1 (Auditing Around The Computer) in Chapter 2. This approach attempts to highlight what may be preserved from the current array of computer auditing techniques. The approach also assumes that auditors would feel comfortable with using CAATS.

AUDIT-APPROACHES TO A COMPUTER-BASED ACCOUNTING SYSTEM IN A SMALL BUSINESS ENVIRONMENT ADVOCATED BY LARGE INTERNATIONAL FIRMS

Approach A

This is a 'top-down' approach. The auditors will consider the extent to which they intend to rely on the client's system in each audit area. It is a systems based approach as opposed to an accounts based approach (i.e. extended substantive testing of the financial statement details). The approach involves the following steps:

1. Carry out a review of general controls. This will include an analysis of whether reliance can be placed on controls, a review of the general controls, tests to see whether they are adequate and an analysis of whether they can be relied on as key controls for a systems based audit. If they can, then the main compliance testing is simplified.

2. This step involves the various stages as identified in Figure A4.1

below. The problem with this approach is that very few micro-computer systems will pass the various stages in which decisions have to be taken. For example to accept a systems based audit one of the following paths has to be followed:

- User controls which are strong enough for reliance to be placed on them will lead to manual compliance testing.
- If there are weak user controls but strong programmed procedures and strong general controls then compliance tests may have to use CAATS, to help in:

    1.   The compliance testing.
    2.   The substantive work.

The two most recommended CAATS are:

Test data: (used for compliance testing i.e. to see whether the system works in the way it is supposed to).

Interrogation packages: (used mainly for substantive tests – though by searching a transaction file, the package can ascertain whether incorrect data can enter the system and this is more of a compliance test).

The problem still remains that minimum standards of general controls are required.

The overall conclusions arising from the evaluation of the internal controls in a small computer environment will often be that audit reliance cannot be placed on them as key controls. Therefore, extended substantive testing of the accounting system and of the financial statements will have to be adopted. The use of CAATS may be cost effective especially where standard enquiry utilities on clients' computers are used for this purpose.

Approach B

This approach starts from the reverse position; i.e., with specific applications controls, and works backwards. However it does assume that general reliance upon all controls for audit purposes is more difficult. The approach therefore, accepts that audit tests are likely to be predominantly of a substantive validation nature.

As well as the substantive testing; internal controls may be studied if:

either   there are situations where controls can be relied upon in particular areas,

or   management require a report on the system of internal controls.

For any business, the auditor determines a strategy for the audit based upon an initial visit to the client and an initial understanding of the systems, the data processing department and the overall management environment. Depending upon the results of this initial work, the auditor will do more or less work on the systems.

The strategy of the auditor is outlined in detail below:

First, he must react specifically in his programme of tests to each significant programmed procedure in the application. The auditor therefore starts by examining what programmed procedures exist and, if they do, whether they can be relied upon (even though such reliance may be difficult because of the absence of general controls).

Second, where it is decided to place reliance on controls for particular applications, the auditor should complete the internal control questionnaire for the application concerned. Where basic controls are considered adequate, compliance tests should be prepared and carried out.

The final task is to carry out compliance tests of the user controls and tests of the programmed procedures. If the results of the tests are such that audit reliance can be placed on the systems, then the auditor can reduce the level of substantive tests.

This must be qualified, however, because there are weaknesses in the discipline exerted over the basic controls (by which we mean weaknesses in those features of the system designed to ensure that the basic controls continue to operate properly and that assets are safeguarded). Because of the weaknesses in these disciplines, the reduction in substantive tests cannot be as great as that possible in a controlled environment with adequate disciplines.

More advanced hardware and software internal controls in a microcomputer environment

HARDWARE SOLUTIONS INVOLVING CURRENT TECHNOLOGY PLUS SOME BESPOKE HARDWARE

A VDU might have the equivalent of three till rolls associated with it to recreate the visible evidence necessary to allow an auditor to check the input into the system under three different headings:

1. Programs run and operating system commands, time of start-up and shut-down and any other operations information including the loading of new programs on to the system for subsequent use.
2. Changes or entry of standing data (plus date and time).
3. Transactions data (plus date and time).

Similarly as an alternative, laser discs (which cannot be erased) could be used to store the same information.

HARDWARE SOLUTIONS INVOLVING NEW TECHNOLOGY

The hardware may incorporate a more severe system with software embedded in the hardware and 'sealed' to guard against software contamination.

Most of the previous solutions are possible with existing hardware or with only minor modifications. The development of the till roll may be classified as an advanced solution, even though we have discussed its use in the previous section. Other more advanced solutions are now considered.

Automatic data capture would prevent human-induced errors and isolate the problem to the incomplete and inaccurate data arising outside the system. There are two particular ways of introducing automatic data capture.

1. Data may be transmitted directly from a cash register. Ideally the price of a good could be magnetically read from a label or code on the product itself, by means of sophisticated point of sale equipment. A sale or other transaction (including 'changing' coins) would be entered into the computer. An error could only arise if a customer were party to it and did not query the transaction or if the goods were sold (or 'bartered') without the transaction being entered through the cash register. In the event of automatic data capture devices, it would be imperative to have a hard copy device or cartridge tape logging the transactions as they occurred.

2. Electronic Funds Transfer Systems are another form of automatic data capture. Invoices could be paid by simultaneously updating:
   (a) The firm's accounts.
   (b) The firm's bank account.
   (c) The supplier's bank account.

To achieve (b) and (c) a telecommunications link to the firm's bank and to the supplier's bank would be required.

However, all cash payments (i.e. equivalent to cheques) would be recorded simultaneously at one or two other locations – the bank(s). The receipt of money paid by a debtor would trigger an entry in the debtor's and cash accounts*. In this way, bank transactions would be duplicated in the firm's computer. This would provide an automatic data capture for cash payments to the firm and a redundancy check between the bank and the firm.

Automatic data capture can only be eluded by cash transactions or through barter.

ADVANCED SOFTWARE SOLUTIONS

There are two types of advanced software which may be useful, assuming that databases and computer audit interrogation facilities are already present.

Abstract data types allow the specification in program compilation of data types with certain attributes. For example, a variable representing a date must comprise three different numbers, the first being an integer between 1 and 31, the second between 1 and 12 and the third between 82 and 99 (with suitable conditions for short months).

With an advanced programming language that allows abstract data types, these conditions are compiled into the program; any data not

---

*In these circumstances we would need a single set of account numbers for both debtors and creditors.

meeting the conditions would create an error. This error would be similar to the input of a real number into an integer variable in current programming languages. The advantage of using abstract data types is that they introduce automatic controls which are beyond even the programmer.

A second powerful tool is referred to in the computer literature as the missing data problem or the automatic auditing of records. There are two relevant situations:

1. If there is an invalid, blank or missing piece of data in a record, an attempt should be made to estimate the value of the missing data (e.g. salary in an employee record).
2. The detection of possible errors that might exist in the records where there is a data-integrity problem.

Some of the approaches require *a priori* knowledge of the data. Lee et al (1978) require no *a priori* knowledge of the data. Through the use of multi-key sorting of records into similar groups (a concept which is precisely defined mathematically) and by using path theory and cluster analysis, an algorithm to estimate missing data and an algorithm to detect possible errors can be devised. More research may have to be carried out in this area but it appears to be a feasible area for further development.

APPENDIX 6

Details of a representative set of accountancy practices visited during the course of the project

PRACTICE 1

The firm is based in a rural county with 14 partners and eight offices spread over a thirty mile radius. Approximately 120 staff are employed of whom 95 could be classified as technical. The firm supports about 20 qualified staff including partners. Gross annual fees are in the region of £1million.

The work undertaken by the partnership can be summarised proportionately by gross fees into the following categories:

Bookkeeping and Accounts Preparation	35%
Auditing	10%
Taxation (personal and corporate)	40%
Executorship, trust and liquidations	15%

The majority of work is concerned with accounts preparation and taxation of sole traders, partnerships and farmers. Only a small amount of auditing is being carried out. This accounts for the relatively low proportion of qualified staff in the partnership and its dependence on clerical and trainee staff. Many of the fees charged to clients are under £1,000 with some fees for personal taxation in the £100 to £200 range.

PRACTICE 2

This firm is based in a county town with one head office and four other offices located within a 20-mile radius. The firm has 9 partners and approximately 150 staff of whom 120 are technical with about 20 qualified accountants, not including the partners. Gross annual fees are in the region of £750,000.

Work performed by the practice can be categorised under the following headings:

Bookkeeping and Accounts Preparation	30%
Auditing	20%
Taxation	25%
Executorship, trust and liquidations	25%

Approximately 30 per cent of the work is agricultural with 20 per cent in the manufacturing and industrial area and 25 per cent in the retail and wholesale trade. In the branch offices of the firm, as much as 50 per cent of the work may be for agricultural clients, with each typically farming 500-600 acres. Such clients would employ an element of secretarial assistance and provide some accounting records. These would normally be in the form of a cashbook and ledger to record VAT, although some farms may keep sales and purchase ledgers, particularly the latter, for internal costing purposes.

PRACTICE 3

This firm is in London and classifies itself as a large medium practice. There are 14 partners and 102 staff. The gross fees are approximately £2m.

The work can be split (according to fee income) into the following areas:

Pure audit	10%
Preparing accounts and auditing for limited liability companies	50%
Preparing accounts and undertaking tax work for non-limited liability businesses	40%

In the latter category a large section are 'entertainment' clients (around 2,500). A typical fee would be £120-£150. The main business revolves around a direct partner-client relationship.

The pure audit work involves three public companies which evolved from family businesses and were looked after by the practice during the transitional period prior to share flotation. The pure audit work assumes a complete set of records and the practice aims for a high auditing standard.

The preparation of accounts and audit of limited liability companies assumes that there is some sort of complete record. A typical client may be a factory with a turnover of £300,000 and net profits of £20,000. A typical fee would be in the range of £500 to £2,500. A senior and junior would normally take around two weeks to complete the work.

PRACTICE 4

There are 9 partners in this practice based in the suburbs of London. The gross fees are substantially greater than £1m.

The work can be split (according to fee income) into the following areas:

Auditing and annual accounts	40%
Management accounts, periodic accounts, contract PAYE and other data processing functions	10%
Recurring tax work,	30%
of which: personal tax work – 20%	
corporate tax work – 10%	
Tax and financial advice of a non-recurring nature aimed at a particular industrial area	20%

There are roughly 600 accounting and auditing clients and 1,400 personal tax clients. Of the 600 accounting and auditing clients, approximately half are limited companies. This comprises mainly large and small family companies, but also includes a number of smaller UK subsidiaries of sizeable foreign-owned companies. Approximately 25 represent major concerns (i.e. annual turnover in excess of £5m) of which not more than half a dozen represent pure audits. It can be assumed that 300 of the accounting clients are partnerships or sole traders, many of which have incomplete records.

The firm has been heavily computerised for several years.

In addition to the nine partners, there are 65 other staff comprising 45 technical staff and 20 secretarial and clerical staff. Of the 45 technical staff:

15 are trainees in various stages of studentship.

18 are qualified staff (ACA or equivalent).

7 are IAS people (or equivalent).

5 are of varying ability and go through to trial balance and even final accounts stages.

To enable students to learn how to carry out incomplete records work effectively, it has been found necessary for them to be trained initially in manual book-keeping as well as in computer applications.

The average charge for incomplete records work is £400.

The firm is worried about administration costs, as overheads have gone up in real terms. The firm is therefore in the final stages of computerising much of the administration and is about to commence micro-filming, back-up filing and storage.

PRACTICE 5

The practice is based in a provincial town and comprises one partner working from one office. The firm employs 5 technical staff in addition to the partner, and two non-technical staff. Gross annual fees are less than £100,000.

The work undertaken by the firm can be broadly classified as follows:

Bookkeeping and Accounts Preparation	70%
Auditing	Negligible
Taxation	15%
Company secretarial work, advice, etc	15%

The majority of work undertaken by the practice is the provision of specialised accounting services for small concerns who either are unable to or choose not to maintain accounting functions themselves. Examples of the service provided are the preparation of VAT returns and preparation of annual accounts.

PRACTICE 6

This is a one partner firm on the outskirts of London. The gross fees are less than £50,000.

The work can be split up (according to fee income) in the following proportions:

Accountancy and tax (normally undertaken together)	93% +
Accountancy/secretarial and record keeping functions	1 or 2%
Audit (of unions, religious organisations, residents' associations and a few very small companies)	5%

The accountancy and tax work is very much concerned with providing a reliable secretarial service.

The practice employs, in addition to the partner, 2 part- time secretaries and 2 students training for ACCA who have A levels and have undergone 9 months' training at a polytechnic.

The two students do most of the routine accounting and secretarial work, such as trial balance, sales ledgers, reconciliations, VAT and wages. The charge for personal tax is £50+, while the charge for incomplete records work is £200+.

There is no computerisation or mechanisation in the firm.

Bibliography

The Accounting Standards Steering Committee, ED18, ICAEW 1977.

The Accounting Standards Steering Committee, ED24, ICAEW 1979.

Adams, D., Computer Security Hardware Devices and Services – I, *EDPACS*, March 1977, pp.1–10.

Adams, D., Computer Security Hardware Devices and Services – II, *EDPACS*, July 1977, pp.10–16.

Adams, D. and Mullarkey, J. F., A Survey of Audit Software, *Journal of Accountancy*, September 1972, pp.39–66.

AICPA, Statement on Auditing Standards No.3: The Effects of EDP on the Auditor's Study and Evaluation of Internal Control, New York, AICPA, 1974.

AICPA, Audits of Service-Center-Produced Records, New York, AICPA, 1974.

AICPA Audit Committee, Advanced EDP Systems and the Auditor's Concerns, *Journal of Accountancy*, January 1975.

AICPA Computer Services Executive Committee, Computer-Assisted Audit Techniques, New York, AICPA, 1977.

AICPA, The Auditor's Study and Evaluation of Internal Control in EDP Systems, New York, AICPA, 1977.

AICPA, Management Control and Audit of Advanced EDP Systems, New York, AICPA, 1977.

AICPA, *Audit Considerations in Electronic Funds Transfer Systems*, New York, AICPA, 1979.

AICPA, Report of the Special Advisory Committee on Internal Accounting Control, New York, AICPA, 1979.

AICPA, *Controls Over Using and Changing Computer Programs*, New York, AICPA, 1979.

AICPA, Audit and Control Considerations in a Minicomputer or Small Business Computer Environment, New York, AICPA, 1981.

Akresh, A. D. and Goldstein, M., -pont-of-Sale Accounting Systems: Some Implications for the Auditor, *Journal of Accountancy*, December 1978, pp.68–74.

Alexander, M. J., *Information Systems Analysis: Theory and Application*, Chicago, Science Research Associates, 1974.

Allen, B., The Biggest Computer Frauds: Lessons for CPAS, *Journal of Accountancy*, May 1977, pp.52–62.

Alter, S. L., *Decision Support Systems: Current Practices and Continuing Challenges*, Reading, Mass., Addison-Wesley, 1980.

Anderson, F. A., The Usefulness of 'Advanced' EDP Audit Techniques, *Journal of Accountancy*, May 1978.

Anderson, L. K., Hendershot, R. A. and Shoonmaker, R. C., Self-Checking Digit Concepts, *Journal of Systems Management*, September 1974, pp.36–42.

American Federation of Information Processing Societies, AFIPS System Review Manual on Security, Montvale, NJ, AFIPS Press, 1974.

Anderson, R. G., *Data Processing and Management Information Systems*, Plymouth, McDonald and Evans, 1974.

Antonelli, D. C., The Role of the Operator in the Supermarket and Retail Store Systems, *IBM Systems Journal*, vol.14, no.1, 1975, pp.34–45.

Arthur Andersen, A Guide for Studying and Evaluating Internal Accounting Controls, Chicago, Arthur Andersen, 1978.

Ashby, W. R., *Introduction to Cybernetics*, London, Methuen University Paperbacks, 1964.

Ashton, F., *Mechanical Accounting*, Plymouth, McDonald and Evans, 1973.

Ashton, R., An Experimental Study of Internal Control Judgments, *Journal of Accounting Research*, Spring 1974 pp.143–157.

Aspinall, D. (ed.), *The Microprocessor and its Application*, Cambridge, Cambridge University Press, 1978.

Aston, E., Micro-computers – a work measurement application in *Management Services*, March 1982.

Atkinson, W. J. and Sanctis, P. A., *Introduction to VSAM*, NJ, Hayden, 1980.

Attwood, F. A. and de Paula, F. C., *Auditing Standards from Discussion Drafts to Practice*, ICAEW, 1978.

✳Auditing Practices Committee of CCAB, *Auditing Standards and Guidelines*, London, ICAEW, 1980.

✳Auditing Practices Committee, *Auditing Guidelines: Auditing in a Computer Environment*, Auditing Practices Committee, January 1982.

Awad, E. M. and Data Processing Management Association, *Automatic Data Processing: Principles and Procedures*, Englewood Cliffs, NJ, Prentice-Hall, 1973.

Baer, R. M., *Digital Villain*, Reading, Mass., Addison-Wesley, 1972.

Bailey, A. D., Internal Accounting Controls in the Office of the Future, *Computer*, May 1981.

Ballam, A., The Key to Successful Use of Micros in *Management Accounting*, March 1982.

Barden, W. Jnr., *How to Buy and Use Minicomputers and Microcomputers*, Indianapolis, Howard W. Sams, 1976.

Barden, W. Jnr., *Microcomputers for Business Applications*, Indianapolis, Howard W. Sams, 1979.

Barker, C., The Existing State of the Art, in *Public Finance and Accountancy*, May 1979.

Barnes, S. H. and Bariff, M. L., Professionalism and the EDP auditor, *The EDP Auditor*, Winter 1978, pp.4–11.

Baxter, W. T., *Accounting Values and Inflation*, Maidenhead, McGraw Hill, 1975.

Benbasat, I. and Dexter, A. S., Value and Events Approaches to Accounting, *The Accounting Review*, October 1979.

Benbasat, I. and Dexter, A. S., Information System Skill Needs of Professional Accountants, *MAS Communication*, October 1982.

Benjamin, R. I., *Control of the Information System Development Cycle*, New York, John Wiley, 1971.

Bentley, T., What Microtechnology Means for the Management Accountant, *Management Accounting* (UK), March 1980.

Berk, M. A., Dunbar, C. W. and Hobson, G. C., Design and Performance Considerations for the Retail Store System, *IBM Systems Journal*, vol.14, no.1, 1975, pp.64–80.

Bhaskar, K. N., *Building Financial Models: A Simulation Approach*, Associated Business Press, 1978.

Bhaskar, K. N., Quantitative Aspects of Management Accounting, in *Essays in British Accounting Research* Ed. M. Bromwich and A. G. Hopwood, London, Pitman, 1981.

Bhaskar, K. N., Pope, P. and Morris, R., Financial Modelling with Computers: A Guide for Management, EIU April 1982.

Bhaskar, K N., Wiliams, B. C., Pope, P. and Morris, R., Financial Modelling with a Microcomputer: Software Choice and Hardware Selection, EIU, April 1984.

Bhaskar, K. N. and team, *Innovative Financial Information Systems Based on Modern Database Concepts* for the ESRC, 1984.

Bigg, W. W., *Practical Auditing*, HFL Publishing, 1958.

Bird, E. A., *Electronic Data Processing and Computing for Commercial Students*, London, Heinemann, 1972.

Birkle, J. R. and Yearsley, R., *Computer Applications in Management*, Associated Business Programmes, 1976.

Birtle, W. G., Hawkins, B. D. and Pugh, W. D., Accounting Controls in a Minicomputer Installation, *Journal of Systems Management*, December 1979.

Birtle, W. G., Hawkins, B. D. and Pugh, W. D., How to Evaluate Accounting Controls in a Minicomputer Installation, *Practical Accountant*, August 1980.

Bjork, Jnr, L. A., Generalized Audit Trail Requirements and Concepts for Data Base Applications, *IBM Systems Journal*, vol.14, no.3, 1975, pp.229–245.

Blish, E. A., Computer Abuse: A Practical Use of the AICPA Guide, *EDPACS*,

September 1978, pp.6–12.

Bodnar, G. H., *Accounting Information Systems* and *Solutions Manual*, Boston, Allyn and Bacon, 1980.

Bodnar, G., Reliability Modelling of Internal Control Systems, *The Accounting Review*, October 1975, pp.747–757.

Boehm, B. W., Software and Its Impact: A Quantitative Study, *Datamation*, May 1973, pp.48–59.

Boehm, B. W., McClean, R. K. and Urfig, D. B., Some Experience with Automated Aids to the Design of Large-Scale Reliable Software, IEEE *Transactions on Software Engineering*, March 1975, pp.125–133.

Bolton Report on Small Firms, H.M.S.O. Cmd. 4811, 1971.

Bolton, J. E., The Future of Small Businesses: A Review of Developments since the Committee of Inquiry (1969-71), *Journal of the Royal Society of Arts*, May 1982.

Bourne, S.R., *The UNIX System*, Reading, Mass., Addison-Wesley, 1982.

Boutell, W. S., *Computer-Oriented Business Systems*, Englewood Cliffs, NJ, Prentice-Hall, 1968.

Boutell, W. S., Auditing and Research, *Accounting Research Convocation*, Alabama, University of Alabama, 1975, pp.87–102.

Bowen, J. B. and Welke, W. R. (eds), *Financial Information Systems: Selected Readings*, Boston, Houghton Mifflin, 1968.

Bradbeer, R., *The Personal Computer Book*, Input Two-Nine, 1980.

Breckner, D. and Abel, P., *Principles of Business Programming*, Englewood Cliffs, NJ, Prentice-Hall, 1970.

Brightman, R. W., Luskin, B. J. and Titton, T., *Data Processing for Decision Making*, New York, Macmillan, 1968.

Briston, R. J. and Williams, B. C., The Polarisation of Accountancy Profession, a UK-USA Comparison, AUTA Conference, Dundee 1981.

British Computer Society *Control and Audit of Minicomputer Systems*, London, Heydon, 1981.

Brodie, M. L., On Modelling Behavioural Semantics in Databases *Proc. 1981 International Conference on Very Large Databases*, Cannes, September 1981.

Brooks, F. P. and Iverson, K. E., *Automatic Data Processing*, New York, John Wiley, 1963.

Brooks, F. P. and Iverson, K. E., *Automatic Data Processing: System/360 Edition*, New York, John Wiley, 1963.

Brown, M., Auditors and Computers – Are they talking the same language? *The Accountant*, July 1981.

Browne, P. S. and Steinauer, D. D., A Model for Access Control in E. F. Codd and A. L. Dean (eds.), *Proceedings of the 1971 ACM-SIGFIDET Workshop: Data Description, Access and Control*, New York, Association for Computing Machinery Inc., 1971, pp.241–262.

Burch, Jr. J. G. and Sardinas, Jr. J. L., *Computer Control and Audit: A Total Systems Approach*, New York, John Wiley, 1978.

Burch, Jr. J. G. and Strater, F. R., *Information Systems: Theory and Practice*, New York, John Wiley, 1974.

Burns, D. C. and Loebbecke, J. K., Internal Control Evaluation: How the

Computer Help, *Journal of Accountancy*, August 1975, pp.66-70.

Burton, A. J. and Mills, R. G., *Electronic Computers and their Business Applications*, London, Ernest Benn, 1960.

Butler, J., Computer Operations Audit – Some New Areas, *EDPACS*, June 1974, pp.5–8.

Butterworth, J., The Accounting System as an Information Function, *Journal of Accounting Research*, Spring 1972.

Canadian Institute of Chartered Accountants, Computer Control Guidelines, Toronto, CICA, 1970.

Canadian Institute of Chartered Accountants, Computer Audit Guidelines, Toronto, CICA, 1975.

Cane, A., Small Business Systems: Battleground of the computer sector, *Financial Times*, June 8 1982.

Canning, R. G., The Internal Auditor and the Computer, *EDP Analyzer*, March 1975, pp.1–13.

Canning, R. G., Recovery in Data Base Systems, *EDP Analyzer*, November 1976, pp.1–11.

Capese, R. P. and Posa, J. G. (eds.), *Microprocessors and Microcomputers*, New York, McGraw-Hill, 1981.

Capese, R. P. (ed.), *Personal Computing Hardware and Software Basics*, New York, McGraw-Hill, 1979.

Cargill, W., Minicomputer Control Alternatives, *Bulletin of the Management Advisory Services Section*, vol. 5, nos. 1 and 2, July 1981, American Accounting Association.

Carlson, A., Changing Role of the Auditor, *Journal of Systems Management*, November 1978.

Cash, J., Bailey, A. D. and Whinston, A., A Survey of Techniques for Auditing EDP Based Accounting Information Systems, *The Accounting Review*, October 1977.

Certified Accountants Educational Trust *Computer Data Processing*, Certified Accountants Technical Publication 1973.

Chaiken, B. R. and Perry, W. E., ITF – A Promising Computer Audit Technique, *Journal of Accountancy*, February 1973.

Chambers, A. D., *Computer Auditing*, London, Pitman 1981.

Chambers, A. D., *Internal Auditing*, London, Pitman 1981.

Chambers, A. D., Audit test packs and computer audit programs, in *The Computer Journal*, vol.18 no.2.

Chambers, A. D., Computer fraud and abuse, in *The Computer Journal*, vol.21 no.3.

Chambers, A. D., Current Strategies for Computer Auditing within an Organisation, in *The Computer Journal*, vol.24, no.4, 1981.

Chandy, K. M., Browne, J. C., Dissly, C. W. and Uhrig, W. R., Analytic Models for Rollback and Recovery Strategies in Data Base Systems, *IEEE Transactions on Software Engineering*, March 1975, pp.100–110.

Chandor, A., Graham, J and Williamson, R., *Practical Systems Analysis*, London, Rupert Hart-Davis Educational Publications, 1969.

Chapdelaine, P. A., *Accuracy Control in Source Data Collection* Ohio, HQ Air

Force Logistics Command, Wright Patterson Air Force Base, 1963.

Chartered Institute of Public Finance and Accountancy *Computer Audit Guidelines*, CIPFA, 1978.

CIPFA, *Computer Audit Statement*, CIPFA, July 1981.

Checkland, P., *Systems Thinking, Systems Practice*, Chichester, John Wiley, 1981.

Chen, P. P., The Entity – Relationship Model: Towards a Unified View of Data, *ACM Transactions on Database Systems*, March 1976.

Chervenak, L., Effectiveness Audit – Keeping Electronic Data Processing (EDP) in Line, *Hospital Financial Management*, 24 July 1978.

Clifton, H. D., *Systems Analysis for Business Data Processing*, Business Books, 1969.

Clifton, H. D., *Business Data Systems: A Practical Guide to Systems Analysis and Data Processing*, London, Prentice-Hall International, 1978.

Clifton, H. D. and Lucey, T., *Accounting and Computer Systems*, London, Business Books, 1973.

Clowes, K. W., Your Client's Computer: A Silent Audit Partner, in *Canadian Chartered Accountant*, August 1980.

Cluff, E. G., *Computerisation for the Small Business*, Input Two-Nine, 1979.

Cohen, J. A., *How to Computerize Your Small Business*, Englewood Cliffs, NJ, Prentice-Hall, 1980.

Colantoni, C., Manes, R. P. and Whinston, A. B., A Unified Approach to the Theory of Accounting and Information Systems, *The Accounting Review*, January 1971.

Collins, S. H., Keeping up with computer technology: an AICPA conference focuses on systems and security, *The Journal of Accountancy*, July 1977.

Colton, K. W. and Kraemer, K. C. (ed.), *Computer and Banking*, New York, Plenum Press, 1980.

Comer, M. J., *Computer Fraud*, London, McGraw-Hill, 1977.

Comptroller General of the United States. *Auditing Computers with a Test Deck*, Washington DC, US Government Printing Office, 1975.

Coopers and Lybrand, *Manual of Auditing*, Wokingham, Gee and Co.

Cowe, R., Auditors come to terms with the computer – at last, *Infomatics*, June 1981.

Crandall, R. H., Information Economics and its Implications for the Further Development of Accounting Theory, *The Accounting Review*, June 1969.

Coughlin, C. W., The Need for Good Procedures, *Journal of Systems Management*, June 1974, pp.30–33.

Court, J. M., *Audit and Control in a Complex Computer Environment*, ICAEW, 1984.

Court, J. M., *The Impact of Computers on the Work of the External Auditor*. Pergamon Infotech State of the Art Report on 'Computer Audit and Control', London, 1980.

Coussins, S., Computer Selection in the Small Business and Medium-size Business, in *Industrial Management+Data Systems*, March/April 1982.

Crowe, T. and Avison, D. E., *Management Information from Databases*, London, Macmillan, 1980.

Crump, D., Computers – what should worry auditors? *Accountancy*, November 1980.

Culbertson, R. C., How Computers Affect Auditing, *Internal Auditor*, February 1978.

Cushing, B. E., *Accounting Information Systems and Business Organizations,* Reading, Mass., Addison-Wesley, 1978.

Cushing, B. E., A Mathematical Approach to the Analysis and Design of Internal Control Systems, *The Accounting Review,* January 1974, pp.24–41.

Cushing, B. E., A Further Note on the Mathematical Approach to Internal Control, *The Accounting Review,* January 1975, pp.151–154.

Cutting, R. W., Guiltman, R. J., Lilly, F. L. and Mullarkey, J. F., Technical Proficiency for Auditing Computer Processed Records, *Journal of Accountancy,* October 1971, pp.74–77.

Date, C., *An Introduction to Database Systems,* 2nd Edition, Reading, Mass., Addison-Wesley, 1977.

Davidson, S., The Day of Reckoning – Managerial Analysis and Accounting Theory, *Journal of Accounting Research* Autumn, 1963.

Davies, C. T., Data Processing Spheres of Control, *IBM Systems Journal,* vol.17, no.2, 1978, pp.179–198.

Davis, G. B., Auditing and EDP, New York, American Institute of Certified Public Accountants, 1968.

Davis, G. B., *Management Information Systems: Conceptual Foundations, Structure and Development,* New York, McGraw-Hill 1974.

Davis, G. B., Adams, D. and Schaller, C. A. Auditing and EDP 2nd ed. New York, American Institute of Certified Public Accountants, 1981.

Davis; G. B. and Weber, R., *Auditing Advanced EDP Systems,* Altamonte Springs, Fla, The Institute of Internal Auditors Inc, 1981.

Davis, J. R. and Cushing, B. E., *Accounting Information Systems,* Reading, Mass., Addison-Wesley, 1980.

Davis, W. S., *Computers and Business Information Processing,* Reading, Mass., Addison-Wesley, 1981.

Davison, I. H., The New Auditing Standards and the Smaller Company, *Accountancy,* April 1979.

Dearnley, P. A., Software Development for Microcomputer Data Processing Systems, *The Computer Journal,* vol.25, no.2, 1982.

Deloitte, Haskins and Sells, *Businessman's Guide to Microcomputers,* London, Deloitte, Haskins and Sells, 1982.

De Marco, T. *Structured Analysis and System Specification,* Englewood Cliffs, NJ, Prentice-Hall, 1978.

De Paula, F. C. and Attwood, F. A., *Auditing: Principles and Practice,* London, Pitman, 1982.

Dock, V. T. and Essick, E., *Principles of Business Data Processing with Basic,* Chicago, Science Research Associates, 1978.

Dorricott, K. O., Appraising Computer Assisted Audit Techniques, *CA Magazine,* August 1975, pp.24–29.

Dorricott, K. O., The Impact of Small Computers on Auditing, *Canadian Management,* January 1979.

Douglas, I. J., *Audit and Control of Mini- and Microcomputers,* Manchester, NCC, 1982.

Dower, R. H., Preparing for the Audit of the Small Computer, *Modern Office and Data Management*, Australia, May 1980.

Drake, R. W. and Smith, J. L., Some Techniques for File Recovery, *The Australian Computer Journal*, November 1971; pp.162–170.

Driver, M. J. and Mock, T. J., Human Information Processing – Decision Style Theory and Accounting Information Systems, *The Accounting Review*, July 1975.

Duff, L. J. and Associates Inc. Montreal, *Security Audit and Control of Small Computer Systems*, Park Ridge, Ill., Bank Administration Institute, 1981.

Earl, M. J., Program Review: Its Role in Computer Auditing, *Managerial Finance*, vol.5, no.2.

Earl, M. J., Program Auditing: A New Approach to Computer Audit, *EDPACS*, December 1977, pp.5–14.

Eaton, J. M. and Hatten, D. J., *Systems Analysis and Computing*, London, Unwin, 1975.

Edwards, C., *Developing Microcomputer-based Business Systems*, London, ICMA, 1982.

Edwards, E and Bell, P., *The Theory and Measurement of Business Income*, University of California Press, Berkeley and Los Angeles, 1961.

EDP Auditors Association Inc., Control Objectives, Hanover Park, Ill., EDP Auditors Association, 1975.

EDP Auditors Foundation for Education and Research, Control Objectives, 2nd edition, Hanover Park, Ill., EDP Auditors Association, 1977.

Ekanadham, K. and Mahjoub, A., Microcomputer Networks, in *The Computer Journal*, vol.24, no.1, 1981.

Eliason, A. L. and Kitts, K. D., *Business Computer Systems and Applications*, Chicago, Science Research Associates, 1979.

Ellison, J. R. and Waring, L. P., Managing Computer Security, *The Accountannt*, July 26, 1979.

Emery, F. E., *Systems Thinking*, Harmondsworth, Penguin 1969.

Evans, C., *The Making of the Micro*, London, Victor Gollancz, 1981.

Everest, G. C. and Weber, R., A Relational Approach to Accounting Models, *The Accounting Review*, April 1977.

Everest; G. C. and Weber, R., Data Base Supported Systems and the Auditing Function, *Auerbach Information Management Series: Data Base Management*, Pennsauken, NJ, Auerbach Publishers, 1977.

Everest; G. C. and Weber, R., Database Administration: Functional, Organizational, and Control Perspectives, *EDPACS*, January 1979, pp.1–10.

Firnberg, D., *Computers, Management and Information*, London, Unwin, 1972.

Fisher, G. H., *Cost Considerations for Systems Analysis* Elsevier, (USA), 1971.

FitzGerald, J., *Internal Controls for Computerized Systems*, San Leandro, Cal., E.M. Underwood, 1978a.

Francis Kinsman Associates-NCC, *Impact of Microprocessors on British Business*, Manchester, NCC, 1979.

Frielink, A. B. (ed.) *Economics of Automatic Data Processing*, Amsterdam, North-Holland Publishing, 1965.

Gallagher, J. D., *Management Information Systems and the Computer*, American Management Association, 1961.

Gear, C. W., *Applications and Algorithms in Business*, Chicago, SRA, 1978.

Gear, C. W., *Computers and Systems*, Chicago, SRA, 1978.

Gemmell, J., Audit Problems Ahead with Small Companies, *Accountancy*, July 1977.

George, F. H., *A Survey of Digital Computing*, Oxford, Pergamon Press, 1968.

Gevirtzman, R., Controls in Automated Information Systems, *Journal of Systems Management*, January 1983.

Gladney, H. M., Worley, E. L. and Myers, J. J., An Access Control Mechanism for Computing Resources, *IBM Systems Journal* vol.14, no.3, 1975, pp.212–228.

Godfrey, J. T. and Prince, T. R., The Accounting Model from an Informations Systems Perspective, *The Accounting Review*, January 1971.

⋇Goossens, B. and Schouten, N., Using the Computer for Audit in *Briefings: Information and Management*, 4, 1981.

Graham, J., *Systems analysis in Business*, London, Unwin, 1972.

Grand, J., Using Computers to Manage Your Cash, *Journal of Systems Management*, January 1983.

Grayston, D., How to Order an Audit *Data Systems*, May 1974.

Greenwald, B. M. and Oberlander, G., IRS Audits of EDP Systems *Management Accounting*, April 1975, pp.13–15.

Gregory, R. H. and van Horn, R. L., *Automatic Data Processing Systems*, London, Chatto and Windus, 1960.

Gregory, R. H. and van Horn, R. L., *Business Data Processing and Programming*, Belmont, Cal., Wadsworth Publishing, 1963.

Grinyer, P. H. and Wooller, J., Corporate Modelling: a new tool for financial management, ICAEW, 1975.

Gross, S. E., Data Center Security, *EDP Auditing* Pennsauken, NJ, Auerbach Publishers Inc., 1978, Portfolio 72–03–03 pp.1–20.

Gustafson, L. M., Improving Relations between Audit and EDP, *EDPACS*, September 1976, pp.1–8.

Hal Reneau J., Auditing in a Database Environment, *Journal of Accountancy*, December 1976.

Hallam, J. A., Hallam, S. F. and Hallam, T. A., Control of MIS: A Comprehensive Model, *Journal of Systems Management*, January 1983.

Hammersley, P., The Impact of Microcomputer Systems on Commercial Data Processing, in *The Computer Journal*, vol.24, no.1, 1981.

Hartman, W., Matthes, H and Proeme, A., *Management Information Systems Handbook: Analysis, Requirements Determination, Design and Development, Implementation and Evaluation*, New York, McGraw-Hill, 1968.

Haseman; W. D. and Whinston, A. B., Design of a Multidimensional Accounting System, *The Accounting Review*, January 1976.

Healey; M., The Possible Impact of Minicomputers and Microprocessors on Mainframe Computer Manufacturers, in *The Computer Journal*, vol.24, no.1, 1981.

Heffer, D. E., King, G. A. and Keith, D., *Basic Principles and Practice of Microprocessors*, London, Edward Arnold, 1981.

Hicks, J. and Leininger, W. E., *Accounting Information Systems*, West Publishing, 1981.

High, J., The Impact of Small Computers on Auditing, *Canadian Chartered Accountant*, January 1979.

Hinde, S. Approaching the first-time computer audit, *Accountancy*, May 1979.

Hislop, I., Evaluating Controls in a Computer-based System, in *Public Finance and Accountancy*, May 1979.

Hodge, R. D., Auditing Micro Systems, *EDPACS*, 1-5 March 1980.

Hoffberg, A. M., Strengthening Controls over Mini- and Microcomputers, *CPA*, May 1980.

Hoffer, J. A., Database Integrity Control *Journal of Systems Management*, August 1977.

Hoffman, L. J., The Formulary Model for Flexible Privacy and Access Controls, *Proceedings of the AFIPS 1971 Fall Joint Computer Conference*, Montvale, NJ, AFIPS Press, 1971, pp.587–601.

Hoffman, L. J., *Modern Methods for Computer Security and Privacy*, Englewood Cliffs, NJ, Prentice-Hall, 1977.

Hohenstein, C. L., *Computer Peripherals for Minicomputers, Microcomputers and Personal Computers*, New York, McGraw-Hill, 1980.

Holley, C. L. and Millar, F., Auditing the On-Line, Real-Time Computer, *Journal of Systems Management*, January 1983.

Hollis, G., The basics of computer security, *Accountancy*, January 1977.

Holmes, F., Auditing from the EDP Manager's Viewpoint, The Internal Auditor, November-December 1975, pp.29–34.

Holmes; G. A New Practice Manual for an Audit Approach to Computers, *Accountancy*, September 1978.

Holmes, G., When a firm buys its own computer system, *Accountancy*, November 1980.

Holmes, J. R., Microcomputer Limitations, *Journal of Accountancy*, December 1979.

Hook, P. E., Computer Auditing – A Growth Industry, *The Accountant*, 26 July, 1979.

Howden, W. E., Reliability of the Path Analysis Testing Strategy, *IEEE Transactions on Software Engineering*, September 1976, pp.208–215.

Hoy, A. B. and Lamond, B. J., An Audit Approach to the Operating System, in *Internal Auditor*, October 1980.

Hubbert, J. F., An Audit of a Realtime System – A Case Study, *EDPACS*, December 1979, pp.1–8.

Hurford, C., Guidelines for Computer Audit, *Public Finance and Accountancy*, April 1980.

IBM Corporation, *Auditability and Productivity Information Catalog*, New York, IBM, 1977.

ICAEW, Manual to course entitled Computer Auditing, ICAEW, 1980.

ICAEW, *On-Line and Distributed Systems* London, ICAEW, 1982.

ICAEW, (AD 121): *Choosing a micro for the Smaller Practice*, Oxley, Summer 1982.

ICAEW, (AD 131): *Audit of Small Computers*, Malcolm and Meadows, Spring 1983.

ICAEW, (AD 139): *Computers for the Practising Accountant*, Edge, Summer 1983.
✕ ICAEW, Proc. Conf. on Auditing in a Computer Environment, 15–17 June 1983.
ICAEW, Information Technology Policy Statement, London, ICAEW 1984.
ICMA *Management Information Systems and the Computer:* Part I Design of a Management Information System, 1967; Part II Computer Applications, 1969; Part II, Section 2 Computer Applications, 1971; Part III Cost effectiveness from Computer Expenditure, 1975; Part IV Cost control and Data Processing Activities, 1978.
Ishikawa, A., A Mathematical Approach to the Analysis and Design of Internal Control Systems: A Brief Comment, *The Accounting Review*, January 1975, pp.148–150.
Ishikawa, A. and Smith, C. H., A Feedforward Control System for Organizational Planning and Control, *Abacus*, December 1972, pp.163–180.
Jahnig, W., The Advent of Automatic Data Processing and the Problems of Auditing with the Aid of ADP, *Management Informatics* vol.3 (1974) no.2.
Jancura, E. G., *Audit and Control of Computer Systems*, New York, Petrocelli/ Charter, 1977.
Jancura, E. G. (ed.) *Computers: Auditing and Control*, 2nd edition, New York, Petrocelli/Charter, 1977.
Jancura, E. G. and Boos, R. J., *Establishing Controls and Auditing the Computerized Accounting System*, New York, Van Nostrand Reinhold, 1981.
Jancura, E. G. and Lilly, F. L., SAS No.3 and the Evaluation of Internal Control, *Journal of Accountancy*, March 1977, pp.69–74.
Jarocki, S. R. and Novotny, E. J., Data Security/Privacy Requirements in Federal Bureaus, *The EDP Auditor*, Summer 1979, pp.35–66.
Jarrett, D., *The Electronic Office*, Aldershot, Gower/Philips Business Systems, 1982.
✕ Jebson, A. and Hepburn, K., Making the computer a useful cost-effective audit tool, *Accountancy*, June 1978.
Jenkins, A. M. and Carlis, J. V., Control Flowcharting for Data Driven systems, *Working Paper MISRC-WP-76-02*, Minneapolis, Minn., Management Information Systems Research Center; University of Minnesota, 1975.
Jenkins, A. and Weber, R., Using DBMS Software as an Audit Tool: The Issue of Independence, *Journal of Accountancy*, April 1976, pp.67–69.
Jenkins, B. G., *External DP Audit Issues and Concerns*, Coopers and Lybrand, 1980.
✕ Jenkins, B. and Pinkney, A., *An Audit Approach to Computers*, ICAEW, 1980.
Jenkins, B. G, The Future Practitioner, proc. con. ICAEW, London, Summer 1983.
Johnson, O., Towards an Events' Theory of Accounting, *The Accounting Review*, October 1970.
Johnson, E. A., *Accounting Systems in Modern Business*, New York, McGraw-Hill, 1959.
Johnson, K. P. and Jaenicke, H. R., *Evaluating Internal Control: Concepts, Guidelines, Procedures, Documentation*, New York, John Wiley, 1980.
Journal of Accountancy, March 1976 Editorial section, Accounting and EDP.
Keen, P. G. W. and Scott Morton, M. S., *Decision Support Systems: An Organizational Pespective*, Reading, Mass., Addison-Wesley, 1978.

Kirschner, L. S., Auditing in a Minicomputer Environment, *EDPACS*, June 1978, pp.1–8.

Kneer, D. C., *Auditing in a Distributed Data Processing Environment: A Model for the Evaluation of Internal Control*, University of Missouri (PhD), 1981.

Knight, B. (ed.), *Guide to Small Business Computers and Word Processing Systems*, Computer Guides Ltd, 1982.

Krause, J. R., Auditing the Integrated Database, *Computerworld*, 18 February 1980.

Krauss, L. I., *Administering and Controlling the Company Data Processing Function*, Englewood Cliffs, NJ, Prentice-Hall, 1969.

Krauss, L. I. and MacGahan, A., *Computer Fraud and Countermeasures*, Englewood Cliffs; NJ, Prentice-Hall, 1979.

Kuong, J. F., *Computer Security, Auditing and Controls*, Wellesley Hills, Mass., Management Advisory Publications, 1974.

Lee, G. W., Re-Thinking Terminal Security Requirements, *EDPACS*, October 1978, pp.138–150.

Lee, R. C. T., Towards Automatic Auditing of Records, in *IEEE Transactions on Software Engineering*, vol.SE-4, no.5, September 1978.

LeGore, L. B., Smoothing Data Base Recovery, *Datamation*, January 1979, pp.177-180.

Lennon, R. E., Cryptography Architecture for Information Security, *IBM Systems Journal*, vol.17, no.2, 1978, pp.138–150.

Lieberman, A. and Whinston, A. B., A Structuring of an Event-Accounting Information System, *The Accounting Review*, April 1975.

Lewis, W. F., Auditing On-Line Computer Systems, in *Journal of Accountancy*, October 1971.

Li, D. H., *Accounting/Computers/Management Information Systems*, New York, McGraw-Hill, 1968.

Lientz, P. B. and Weiss, I. R., *The Vulnerability of Computer Auditing*, California University, Los Angeles Graduate School of Management, 1977.

Litecky, C., *Bulletin of the Management Advisory Services Section*, vol.5, nos. 1 and 2, July 1981, American Accounting Association.

Litecky, C. and Rittenberg, L. E., The External Auditor's Review of Computer Controls, *Computing Practices*, May 1981.

Litecky, C. and Weber, R., The Demise of Generalised Audit Software Packages, *The Journal of Accountancy*, November 1974, pp.45–48.

Loebbecke, J. K. and Zuber, G. R., Evaluating Internal Control, *Journal of Accountancy*, February 1980, pp.49–56.

Loebbecke, J. K., Mullarkey, J. F. and Zuber, G. R. Auditing in a Computer Environment, *Journal of Accountancy*, January 1983.

Lohman, G. M. and Muckstadt, J. A., Optimal Policy for Batch Operations: Backup, Checkpointing, Reorganization, and Updating, *ACM Transactions on Database Systems*, September 1977, pp.209–222.

Losty, P. A., *The Effective Use of Computers in Business*, London, Cassell, 1969.

Lucas, H., The Use of Accounting Information in Decision Making, *The Accounting Review*, July 1975.

Lucas, H., *Computers in Business Studies*, Plymouth, McDonald and Evans, 1973.

Lucas, H.C., *Why Information Systems Fail*, New York, Columbia University Press, 1975.

Lucas, H. C., *The Implementation of Computer-Based Models*, New York, National Association of Accountants, 1976.

Lucas, H. C., *The Analysis, Design and Implementation of Information Systems*, New York, McGraw-Hill, 1976.

Lucas, H. C., *Information Systems Concepts for Management*, New York, McGraw-Hill, 1978.

Lyons, N. R., Segregation of Functions in EFTS, *Journal of Accountancy*, October 1978, pp.89–92.

Mace, R., *Management Information and the Computer*, London, Haymarket Publishing, 1974.

Mackness, J., The Application of Systems Engineering Principles to Operations of Small Companies, Lancaster University Ph.D Dissertation Abstract No. D5117/75.

Madnick, S. E., *Computer Security*, New York, Academic Prsss, 1979.

Mair, W. C., Parallel Simulation – A Technique for Effective Verification of Computer Programs, *EDPACS*, April 1975, pp.1–5.

Mair, W. C., Wood, D. R. and Davis, K. W., *Computer Control and Audit*, 2nd edition, Altamonte Springs, Fla, The Institute of Internal Auditors Inc., 1978.

Mantle, P., The Mood of the Smaller Firms, *The Accounting Bulletin*, June 1983.

Mandell, S. L., *Computers and Data Processing: Concepts and Applications* and Study Guide, St. Paul, West Publishing 1979.

Marsh, R., Making Data More Secure, *Datamation*, October 1976.

Martin, J., *Principles of Database Management*, Englewood Cliffs, NJ, Prentice-Hall, 1967.

Martin, J., *Security, Accuracy, and Privacy in Computer Systems*, Englewood Cliffs, NJ, Prentice-Hall, 1973.

Martin, J., *Future Developments in Telecommunications*, Englewood Cliffs, NJ, Prentice-Hall, 1971.

Martin, J., *Application Development without Programmers*, Englewood Cliffs, NJ, Prentice-Hall, 1982.

Matyas, S. M. and Meyer, C. H., Generation, Distribution and Installations of Cryptographic Keys, *IBM Systems Journal*, vol.17, no.2, 1978, pp.126–137.

Maxson, E. C. and Lyons, N. R., EDP Systems-Designing the Next Generation of Auditing Software, *Internal Auditor*, December 1978.

McAllister, J. P. and Dirsmith, M. W., How the Client's Business Environment Affects the Audit, *Journal of Accountancy*, February 1982.

McCarthy, W. E., A Relational Model for Events-Based Accounting Systems, Dissertation, University of Massachusetts, 1978.

McCarthy, W. E., An Entity-Relationship View of Accounting Models, *The Accounting Review*, October 1979.

McCarthy, W. E. and Gal, G., Declarative and Procedural Aspects of a CODASYL Accounting System, Working Paper 81-2, Michigan University Graduate School of Business Administration, 1981.

McCarthy, W. E., Construction and Use of Integrated Accounting Systems with

Entity-Relationship Modelling, in P.P. Chen (ed.) *Entity-Relationship Approach to Systems Analysis and Design*, Amsterdam, North-Holland Publishing, 1980.

McCarthy, W. E., Multidimensional and Disaggregate Accounting Systems: A Review of the 'Events' Accounting Literature, *Bulletin of the Management Advisory Services Section*, vol.5, nos.1 and 2, July 1981, AAA.

McCarthy, W. E., The REA Accounting Model: A Generalized Framework for Accounting Systems in a Shared Data Environment, *The Accounting Review*, July 1982.

McCosh, A. M., Rahman, M and Earl, M. J., *Developing Managerial Systems*, London, Macmillan, 1981.

McHugh, A. J., EDP and the Audit Function, *Accounting Education*, November 1978, pp.34–54.

McKee, T. E., Auditing Under the Foreign Corrupt Practices Act, *The CPA Journal*, August 1979, pp.31–35.

✔ McKeone, D. H., *Small Computer for Business and Industry*, Aldershot, Gower Publishing, 1979.

McKnight, G., *Computer Crime*, New York, Walker Publishing Company, 1973.

McLeod Jnr., R., *Management Information Systems*, Chicago, Science Research Associates, 1979.

McMillan, C. and Gonzalez, R. F., *Systems Analysis: A Computer Approach to Decision Models*, Richard Irwin, 1965.

McNurlin, B. C., The Automated Office: Part I, *EDP Analyzer*, September 1978, pp.1–13.

McRae, T. W., *The Impact of Computers on Accounting*, London, John Wiley, 1964.

McRae, T. W., *Computers and Accounting*, Lightbown Press, 1976.

McRae, T. W., *A Study of the Application of Statistical Sampling to External Auditing*, London, ICAEW, 1982.

McRae, T. W., *Statistical Sampling for Audit and Control*, Chichester, John Wiley, 1974.

Meng, L. A., The Auditor's Detection Responsibility: Is there an 'Expectation Gap'?, *Journal of Accounting*, October 1980.

Moore, R. A., Rose, B. F., Koger, T. J., Computer Generated Documentation, *Journal of Accountancy*, June 1975, pp.82–86.

Morley, D. W., *Automatic Data Processing*, London, Department of Scientific and Industrial Research, 1961.

Mullen, J. B., Developing an EDP Audit Staff, *EDP Auditing*, Pennsauken, NJ, Auerbach Publishers 1979, Portfolio 71-03-08, pp.1–7.

Murdick, R. G. and Ross, J. E., *Information Systems for Modern Management*, Englewood Cliffs, NJ, Prentice-Hall, 1971.

Murdick, R. G., Fuller, T. G., Ross, J. E. and Winnermark, F. J., *Accounting Information Systems*, Englewood Cliffs, NJ, Prentice-Hall, 1978.

Myers, E., EDP Auditors: Explosive Growth, *Datamation*, August 1977, pp.120–121, 124.

Naylor, T. H., Balintfy, J. C., Burdick, D. S., Chu, K., *Computer Simulation Techniques*, New York, John Wiley, 1966.

NCC, *Introducing Systems Analysis and Design*, Manchester, NCC, 1978.

NCC, *Introducing Data Processing*, Manchester, NCC, 1980.

NCC, *Guidelines for Computer Managers*, Manchester, NCC, 1981.

NCC, *Audit and Control of Mini and Microcomputers*, Manchester, NCC, 1982.

NCC, *Accounting Software Controls a guidance document*, Manchester, NCC, 1983.

Neumann, A. J., *Features of Seven Audit Software Packages – Principles and Capabilities*, Washington DC, US Government Printing Office, 1977, SD Catalog No. C13.10:500–13.

Norman, A., Computer frauds – are they a manageable risk in *Accountancy*, October 1976.

Olney, D. (ed.), Microcomputing for Business: A User's Guide, *Personal Computer World*, London, Century Publishing, 1981.

Olney, D. (ed.), The Microcomputer Handbook: A Buyer's Guide, *Personal Computer World*, London, Century Publishing, 1981.

Online, (ed.), *Microcomputers and Small Business Systems*, Online 1976.

Online, (ed.), *New Concepts in Business Information*, Online 1979.

Online, (ed.), *Micro-systems in Business*, Online, 1980.

Optner, S. L. (ed.), *Systems Analysis*, Harmondsworth, Penguin Books, 1973.

Orilia, L. S., Stern, N., Stern, R. A., *Business Data Processing Systems*, New York, John Wiley, 1972.

Orr, K. T., Systems Design, Structured Programming and Data Security, *IBM Data Security Forum*, September 1974, paper 33.

Osborne, A. and Cook, S., *Business System Buyers' Guide*, Maidenhead, McGraw-Hill, 1981.

Page, J. and Hooper, P., *Accounting and Information Systems*, Englewood Cliffs, NJ, Prentice-Hall, 1979.

Page, M. J., Financial Reporting and the Small Independent Company, for Technical and Research Committee of ICAEW, University of Southampton, June 1981.

Palmer, F. B., Designing the Next Generation of Auditing Software, in *The Internal Auditor*, December 1978.

Palmer, F. B., An Audit Approach to the Operating System, in *The Internal Auditor*, October 1980.

Pannell, B. K., Jackson, D. C. and Lucas, S. B., *Make a Success of Microcomputing in your Business;* London, ICAEW and Enterprise Books, 1983.

Parker, D. B., *Crime by Computer*, New York, Charles Scribner, 1976.

Parker, D. B., *Computer Security Management*, Reston, Virginia, Prentice-Hall, 1981.

Parker, D. B., Nycum, S. and Oura, S. S., Computer Abuse, Stanford, Cal. Stanford Research Institute, 1973.

Patrick, R. L., Auditing and DP: Redressing the Relationship, *Datamation*, 15 November 1978.

Peat, Marwick, Mitchell and Co., *Research Opportunities in Auditing*, New York, Peat, Marwick, Mitchell and Co., 1976.

Pechura, M. A., Microcomputers as Remote Nodes of a Distributed System, *Computing Practices*, November 1981.

Pedder, D. G. (ed.), *Microcomputer Systems in Business*, Aldershot, Gower-BIS Pedder Associates, 1980.

Perkins, B. D., Internal Control for the Small Business, *Management Accounting*, February 1982.

Perry, W. E., Audit Aspects of Utility Programs, *EDPACS*, October 1975, pp.1–8.

Perry, W. E., Management Support for EDP Auditing, *EDPACS*, August 1976, pp.5–9.

Perry, W. E., Using SMF as an Audit Tool – Security, *EDPACS*, January 1976, pp.1–8.

Perry, W. E., Computer Audit Practices, *EDPACS*, July 1977, pp.1–9.

Perry, W. E., Skills Needed to Utilize EDP Audit Practices, *EDPACS*, November 1977b, pp.1–13.

Perry, W. E., The EDP Auditor Relationship with DP Management, *EDP Auditing*, Pennsauken, NJ, Auerbach Publishers, 1978, Portfolio 71-02-03, pp.1–15.

Perry, W. E., Selecting Computer Audit Practices, *EDPACS*, March 1978, pp.1–11.

Perry, W. E. and Adams, D. L., Use of Computer Audit Practices in *EDPACS*, November 1978.

Perry, W. E. and Fitzgerald, J., Designing for Auditability in *Datamation*, August 1977.

Pillsbury, W. F., *Computer Augmented Accounting*, Cincinnati, South Western Publishing, 1971.

Pooch, U. W. and Chattergy, R., *Minicomputers: Hardware, Software and Selection*, St Paul, West Publishing, 1980.

Porter, W. T. and Perry, W. E., *EDP Controls and Auditing*, 2nd edition, Belmont, Cal., Wadsworth Publishing, 1977.

Posner, B. G., Learning to Live with Micros, *INC*, July 1982.

Prakash, P. and Rappaport, A., Informational Interdependencies: System Structure Induced by Accounting Information, *The Accounting Review*, October 1975.

Price Waterhouse, *Accounting Controls in a Minicomputer Installation*, New York, Price Waterhouse, 1979.

Price Waterhouse, *Efficient and Effective Use of CAAT*, Audit Guidance Series, New York, Price Waterhouse, 1981.

Price Waterhouse, *Evaluation and Testing of EDP Controls*, Audit Guidance Series, New York, Price Waterhouse, 1981.

Prince, T. R., *Information Systems for Management Planning and Control*, Illinois, Richard Irwin, 1966.

Pritchard, F. C., Small Business Computers: The Other Solution, *Modern Office and Data Management* (Australia), August 1976.

Pritchard, J., Computer security – what is the auditor's role?, *Accountancy*, November 1978.

Putnam, A. O., *Management Information Systems*, London, Pitman, 1977.

Raiborn, D. D., *Audit Problems encountered in Small Business Engagements*, AICPA, 1982.

Ramamoorthy, C. V., Ho, S. F. and Chen, W. T., On the Automated Generation of Program Test Data, *IEEE Transactions on Software Engineering*, December 1976, pp.293–300.

Reid, G. F. and Demcak, J. A., EDP Audit Implementation with General Purpose Software, *Journal of Accountancy*, July 1971.

Reynolds, P. D., *A Computer ABC*, London, ICAEW, 1965.

Richardson, D. R., Auditing EFTS, *Journal of Accountancy*, October 1978, pp.81–87.

Rittenberg; L. E., The Impact of Internal Auditing during the EDP Application Design Process on Perceptions of Internal Audit Independence, Unpublished Ph.D. dissertation, University of Minnesota; Minneapolis, Minn., 1975.

Rittenberg, L. E. and Davis, G. B., The roles of internal and external auditors in auditing EDP systems, *The Journal of Accountancy*, December 1977.

Robinson, L. A., Davis, J. R. and Alderman, C. W., *Accounting Information Systems: A Cycle Approach*, San Francisco, Harper and Row, 1982.

Roberts, R., Impact on the Auditor of Recent Developments Relating to Internal Control, *The EDP Auditor*, Winter 1978, pp.12–20.

Roberts, R., Microprocessors and Small Business: Risks and Opportunities for the Public Accountant, in *National Public Accountant*, September 1979.

Rocke, M. G., The Need for Data Code Control, *Datamation*, September 1973, pp.105–108.

Rosa, N. and S., *Small Computers for the Small Businessman*, Oregon, Dilithium Press, 1980.

Ruder, B. and Madden, J. D., *An Analysis of Computer Security Safeguards for Detecting and Preventing Intentional Computer Misuse*, Washington DC, Institute for Computer Sciences and Technology, National Bureau of Standards, 1978, Report No. C13.10:500-25.

Saiady, C. and Stokes, A. V. (ed.), *What to Read in Micro-computing: A Selective Bibliography with Annotations*, Aldershot, Gower, 1982.

Sanders, D., *Computers in Business*, Tokyo, McGraw-Hill Kogakusha, 1979.

Sanders, N., *The Corporate Computer*, London, McGraw-Hill, 1973.

Sanders, N., *The St. Merino Solution*, Associated Business Programmes, 1978.

Santocki, J., *Case Studies in Auditing*, Plymouth, McDonald and Evans, 1972.

Sardinis; J., Burch, J. G. and Asebrook, R., *EDP Auditing: A Primer*, New York, John Wiley, 1981.

Savich, R. S., The Use of Accounting Information in Decision Making, *The Accounting Review*, July 1977.

Sawyer, L. B., *The Practice of Modern Internal Auditing*, Altamonte Springs, Fla., The Institute of Internal Auditors, 1973.

Sayani, H. H., Restart and Recovery in a Transaction-Oriented Information Processing System in Randall Rustin (ed.) *ACM SIGMOD Workshop on Data Description, Access and Control*, New York, Association for Computing Machinery 1974, pp.351–366.

Schaller, C. A., Auditing and Job Accounting Data, *Journal of Accountancy*, May 1976, pp.36–42.

Schaller, C. A., The Revolution of EFTS, *Journal of Accountancy*, October 1978, pp.74–80.

Scherf, J. A., Computer and Data Security: A Comprehensive Annotated Bibliography, in *Data Security and Data Processing Volume 4 Study Results: MIT*, New York, IBM, 1974, pp.223–300.

Semprevivo, P.C. *Systems Analysis: Definition, Process and Design*, Chicago, Science Research Associates, 1976.

Senn, J. A., A Management View of Systems Analysts: Failures and Short-comings, *Management Information Systems Quarterly*, September 1978, pp.25–32.

Shannon, C. E. and Weaver, W., *The Mathematical Theory of Communication*, University of Illinois, 1949.

Sharratt, J. R., *Data Control Guidelines*, Manchester (UK), NCC Publications, 1974.

Shave, M. J. R., *Data Structures*, London, McGraw-Hill, 1975.

F Shave, M. J. R. and Bhaskar, K. N., *Computer Science applied to Business Systems*, London, Addison-Wesley, 1982.

Shearon, W., Butler, C. and Benjamin, J., Audit Aspects of Small Computer Systems, *CPA*, August 1980.

Sherwood, D., Financial Modelling, *ICAEW* (AD 153) Winter 1983–4.

Shore, B., A Microcomputer-based Purchasing Information System, *Journal of Purchasing and Materials Management*, Summer 1981.

Short, G. E., Threats and Vulnerabilities in a Computer System, *Data Security and Data Processing Volume 5 Study Results: TRW Systems Inc*, New York, IBM, 1974, pp.25–73.

Simpson, R., An Exercise in Computer Security, *Public Finance and Accountancy*, May 1979.

Simpson, W. D., Luecke, G., Cannon, D. L. and Clemens, D. H., *Microprocessors/Microcomputers/Systems Design*, New York, Texas Instruments/McGraw-Hill, 1980.

F Sippl, C. J. and Dahl, F., *Computer Power for Small Business*, Englewood Cliffs, NJ, Prentice-Hall, 1979.

Skelcher, D., *Word Processing Equipment Survey*, Online, 1982.

Skinner, R. M. and Anderson, R. J., *Analytical Auditing*, Toronto, Sir Isaac Pitman, 1966.

F Smolin, C. R., *How to Buy the Right Small Business Computer System*, New York, John Wiley, 1981.

Sorter, G. An Events Approach to Accounting Theory, *The Accounting Review*, April 1969.

Stanford Research Institute, Systems Auditability and Control Study: Data Processing Audit Practices Report, Altamonte Springs, Fla., The Institute of Internal Auditors, 1977.

State of Illinois, Elements and Economics of Information Privacy and Security, *Data Security and Data Processing Volume 3 Part 2 Study Results: State of Illinois*, New York, IBM, 1974, pp.23–244.

State of Illinois, Recommended Security Practices, *Data Security and Data Processing Volume 3 Part 2 Study Results: State of Illinois*, New York, IBM, 1974, pp.245–380.

Stepczyk, F. M., Requirements for Secure Operating Systems, *Data Security and Data Processing Volume 5 Study Results: TRW Systems Inc*, New York, IBM, 1974 pp.75–205.

Sterling, T. D., Consumer Difficulties with Computerized Transactions: An Empirical Investigation, *Communications of the ACM*, May 1979, pp.283–289.

Stoneham, M. W., Database Auditing – A New Complexity, in *Canadian Chartered Accountant*, May 1979.

Sykes, D. J., Protecting Data by Encryption, *Datamation*, August 1976, pp.81, 84–85.

Szpiro, L., A Microcomputer as a Production Tool for Internal Work by a Statutory Auditor, *Data Processing and Information*, Paris, 15–19 September 1980.

Talbot, J. R., *Management Guide to Computer Security*, Aldershot, Gower, 1981.

Tatham, L., Computer systems and the accountant, *Accountancy*, September 1973.

Thackray, R., A Practical Approach to Computer Audit, in Public *Finance and Accountancy*, May 1979.

Thierauf, R. J., *Decision Support Systems for Effective Planning and Control: A Case Study Approach*, Englewood Cliffs, NJ, Prentice-Hall, 1982.

Thomas, A. J. and Douglas, I. J., *Audit of Computer Systems*, Manchester, NCC 1981.

UEC., Draft Auditing Statement No.13, Union des Experts Comptables et Financiers, January 1982.

F University of Lancaster, Department of Marketing *Small Computers for Small Companies*, Lancaster, University of Lancaster, 1982.

Vance, L. L., Boutell, W. S., *Principles of Auditing*, Illinois, Dryden Press, 1975.

Vanderlee, P., Small Business – An EDP Audit Can Keep your Mini from Becoming a Nightmare, *Canadian Business*, October 1980.

Van Tassel, D. *Computer Security Management*, Englewood Cliffs, NJ, Prentice-Hall, 1972.

Veit, S. S., *Using Microcomputers in Business: A Guide for the Perplexed*, NJ, Hayden, 1981.

Verhofstad, J. S. M., Recovery Techniques for Database Systems, *Computing Surveys*, June 1978, pp.167–195.

F Vincent, D., The Impact of Computers on Small Firms (Accounts Data Processing), *Computer Weekly*, 7 October 1976.

Webb, R. D., Audit Planning–EDP Consideration, *Journal of Accountancy*, May 1979.

Weber, R., *EDP Auditing: Conceptual Foundations and Practice*, New York, McGraw-Hill, 1982.

Weber, R., An Audit Perspective of Operating System Security, *Journal of Accountancy*, 140, September 1975, pp.97–100.

Weber, R., Auditing Computer Systems Using Integrated Test Facility, *The Australian Accountant*, May 1975, pp.232–235.

Weber, R., Audit Capabilities of Some Database Management Systems, *Working Paper MISRC-WP-75-05* MISRC, University of Minnesota, Minneapolis, Minn. 1975.

Weber, R., Implications of Database Management Systems for Auditing Research, in Barry E. Cushing and Jack L. Krogstad (eds.), *Studies in Accounting No.7: Frontiers of Auditing Research*, Texas, Bureau of Business Research, The University of Texas at Austin, 1977.

Weber, R., Auditor Decision Making on Overall System Reliability: Accuracy, Consensus, and the Usefulness of a Simulation Decision Aid, *Journal of Accounting Research*, Autumn 1978, pp.368–388.

✳ Weber, R., On Some Aspects of Audit Software Attributes and User Needs, *Proceedings of the Eighth Australian Computer Conference*, Canberra, Australian Computer Society, 1978, pp.1781–1794.

✳ Weber, R., Audit Trail System Support in Advanced Computer-Based Accounting Systems, *The Accounting Review*, April 1982.

Weiss, H., Audit Review of Program Code-II, *EDPACS*, August 1975; pp.6–7.

Weston, S. S., Program Library Control and Security, *EDPACS*, September, 1979, pp.1–9.

Wilkins, T., Computer Fraud: Implications for the Accounting Profession, *Journal of Accounting*, October 1980.

Wilkinson, B., Controlling Output Distribution, *EDP Auditing*, Pennsauken, NJ, Auerbach Publishers, 1978, Portfolio 74-02-01, pp.1–12.

✳ Wilkinson, B., Selecting Audit Software, *EDP Auditing*, Pennsauken, NJ, Auerbach Publishers, 1978, Portfolio 73-01-04, pp.1–12.

Will, H. J., Discernible Trends and Overlooked Opportunities in Audit Software, *The EDP Auditor*, Winter 1978, pp.21–45.

F Willis, E., A Step by Step Approach to Introducing Computer Technology into Small and Medium Sized Firms, in *Management Decision*, vol.29, no.3, 1981.

Wilson Committee Interim Report on the Financing of Small Firms, Norwich, H.M.S.O. Cmnd 7503, 1979.

✳ Wooldridge, S., *Software Selection*, Philadelphia, Auerbach Publishers, 1973.

Yu, S. and Neter, J., A Stochastic Model of the Internal Control System, *Journal of Accounting Research*, Autumn 1973, pp 273–295.

Zimmerman, H., Minis Lend Themselves to DP Crime, *Computerworld*, 4 September 1978.

Index

Page numbers given in *italics* indicate that information will be found in tabulated form.